Two Generations on the Allegheny Portage Railroad

The First Railroad to Cross the Allegheny Mountains

To Kelvin Happy Birthday 2013 from Penny & Jerry

by

Chris J. Lewie

BURD STREET PRESS
SHIPPENSBURG, PENNSYLVANIA

Photos are the author's unless otherwise noted.

The acid-free paper used in this book meets the guidelines for permanence and durability of the Committee on Production Guidelines for Book Longevity of the Council on Library Resources.

For a complete list of available publications
please write
Burd Street Press
Division of White Mane Publishing Company, Inc.
P.O. Box 708
Shippensburg, PA 17257-0708 USA

Library of Congress Cataloging-in-Publication Data

Lewie, Christopher J., 1963-
    Two generations on the Allegheny Portage Railroad : the first railroad to cross the Allegheny Mountains / by Christopher J. Lewie.
        p. cm.
    Includes bibliographical references and index.
    ISBN-13: 978-1-57249-257-8 ISBN-10: 1-57249-257-0 (alk. paper)
    1. Allegheny Portage Railroad--History. 2. Railroads--Pennsylvania--History. I. Title.

TF25.A35 L49 2001
385'.6'097487--dc21

                                                                2001029507

PRINTED IN THE UNITED STATES OF AMERICA

This book is dedicated to my wife, Regina,
who has been very supportive of my earthly endeavors,
who has listened, and been part of all my dreams.
Thanks again, Honey!

Contents

Preface

The only actual steam locomotive I ever saw was the American Freedom Train during a nationwide tour in 1975, when I was in the fifth grade. The engine was a rebuilt 1941 Reading T-1 coal-burning locomotive with a bright "1" painted on the front. The shiny black "steamer" weighed four hundred tons, and I had never seen anything in the world that large. Following the engine were a dozen red, white, and blue cars filled with the nation's treasures of over two hundred years of American history. In retrospect, it was quite an adventure for an impressionable 12-year-old kid, so I guess you can say that this book actually began right there on that spring day during the Bicentennial celebration.

Twenty-four years later, I gave a speech at the Allegheny Portage Railroad National Historic Site in Gallitzin, Pennsylvania, about my mother's family who had lived in the area and worked on the Allegheny Portage Railroad. Several of the participants mentioned to me afterward what a great subject this would be for a book. A book about my family who worked on the railroad? I was flattered but didn't think so. It sounded too boring—even to me. I didn't really give it much thought since I was not a professional writer or a train buff, and the last seven years of research were just an enjoyable genealogical project. But, the more I thought about it, the more I realized there was something worth writing about. I modified my family story to include as many aspects as possible about the Allegheny Portage RR between the years 1832–1857. This book, and their story, is that end result.

Acknowledgments

The author would like to acknowledge the following institutions and people for their assistance:

Cambria County Historical Society, especially the assistance of Ms. Leslie Conrad, curator. This is where many of the old local newspaper articles from the time period 1825–1857 are located. Without their immense resources and Leslie's help, this book would probably not have been possible.

Allegheny Portage Railroad National Historic Site, for providing expertise on the operation of the Allegheny Portage RR and photos of the Summit Mansion House. Special thanks to park rangers Diane Garcia and Nancy Smith for their assistance and the opportunity for me to share what I have found with their "Evenings at the Summit," in July 1999.

Blair County Historical Society, especially the assistance of Mr. Tim Van Scoyoc, acting director/curator. Located in the Baker Mansion in Altoona, it is an immense resource and storehouse of material from the Portage RR and early canal days such as old newspapers, Summit Mansion hotel ledgers, "Riffle & Humphreys Merchants" papers, and others. The restored Baker Mansion exhibits an excellent historical perspective of this unique pre-Civil War period in American history.

Railroaders Memorial Museum, for photos of the famous Horseshoe Curve and Gallitzin Tunnels. Thanks to Ms. Jan Hartman, curator.

Pennsylvania State Archives, for providing thousands of pages of information from the Pennsylvania Main Line canal days and resources including the individual payroll sheets and contracts from the Allegheny Portage RR from the 1830s to the 1850s. I looked through six thousand paper records in three days.

The inventor of the personal computer, without my old trusty Apple-Macintosh I could not have completed this work. Thanks "Silicon Valley"!

And, all those individuals who have ever supported my research into the history of the Humphreys family in Pennsylvania and Ohio during the 1990s, including my aunt Mary (Durfee) Kirwin and her mother, my maternal grandmother, Ann Louise (Humphreys) Kirwin (1913–1997), who shared her personal knowledge of her forefathers with me, to be shared with future generations. Grandma Kirwin died prior to the publication of this book. This book is in her honor!

Introduction

During the early to mid-1800s, the railroad began to dominate not only the transportation industry but the very economy of America as well. Entire towns and communities lived and died with the fortunes of these transportation giants. Summitville in eastern Cambria County was one such town. This remote mountain community found itself at the forefront of railroading technology in the early 1830s. This was brought about by a need by the Allegheny Portage Railroad (part of the Pennsylvania Main Line Canal System) to compete with the Erie Canal to the north and the Chesapeake & Ohio Canal to the south for the lucrative western freight traffic. The Allegheny Portage Rail-Road, one of the first railroads in the country, was not just a part of the industrial age — it was the beginning of the great transportation revolution in America.

What follows is the story of two generations of a family who became caught up in the middle of this technological, economic, and political struggle. By using newspaper articles of the day and historical documents, a picture emerges illustrating their struggle to cope in an ever-changing world driven by steam technology.

Chapter One
The Cambrians

When Rowland Humphreys, a Welshman, came to America there was no such thing as a railroad. By the time he was killed in 1852, he and his family had become involved in the most controversial railroad in the country. Rowland was born in 1795 in or near the town of Llanbrynmair, located within the midst of the Cambria Mountains of central Wales. The Cambrian Mountains run north to south through Wales with the highest peak about 2,500 feet above sea level and at a latitude from 52 to 53 degrees north. Because of their cool, wet climate, the Cambrian Mountains were perfect for grasslands and grazing and became the home of hardy sheep farmers.

During the late 1700s, there was a great religious and intellectual movement in Wales to make everyone literate. Becoming literate was equated with holiness; reading the Bible made for better Christians; becoming better Christians created better citizens. However, instructors of these studious Christian churches did not realize that once you could read—you would become interested in reading anything else such as newspapers, books, political posters, and maps; even from far away places like America.

In 1811, the Methodists in Wales broke away from the Church of England and created a "non-conformist nation." A nationwide farm crisis and population explosion occurred simultaneously in 1815, placing enormous pressure on local resources. The years 1815–1848 were characterized by a period of social unrest, with the Catholics in Cambria in the middle of the turmoil. Some Cambrians old enough to understand these economic, social, religious, and political problems, yet young enough to leave everything

1

they have ever known behind, decided to sail across the Atlantic Ocean for the American frontier. Among this host of young men was Rowland Humphreys.

Young Humphreys, with a group of fellow Welshmen, arrived at the wild front range of the Allegheny Mountains in western Pennsylvania around 1815. They immigrated directly to a location named, of all things, "Cambria County." Cambria County was not named by chance. The previous Welsh immigrants, who were among the first wave of foreign immigrants to this portion of Pennsylvania during the late 1700s, named it. They also created a small town called Ebensburg just west of Allegheny Mountain near the headwaters of the Conemaugh River. To them, the rugged mountainous outpost resembled their homeland back in Wales, and thus the name "Cambria" was correctly conferred upon the area. The Allegheny Mountain range ran north to south and was the backbone of the West. Its highest elevation reached 2,500 feet and was ideal for grazing sheep after the timber was cut down and used for building farms and homesites. The newfound country appeared like home to the immigrants, but without the social and political problems of a nonconformist nation or the British government. Reverend Rhys (sometimes spelled "Rees") declared that this was the place to start a colony of Welshmen in an English-speaking country. It was an ambitious adventure.

In Cambria County, most of the roads were old Indian trails and cart paths through the mountains, barely upgraded for coaches or wagons. Even within the county, Ebensburg, the county seat, was isolated from Johnstown except for a treacherous mountain path. It could take a whole day to travel 15 miles up and down the mountains and the ravines. Every stream crossing was an adventure—even in good weather. The Indiana, Huntingdon, & Cambria Turnpike would open up this remote county with a road for commerce that was wide, sturdy, and direct. The selected route went right through Cambria County and Ebensburg to Indiana County. The only other form of heavy travel in or out of the county was by water on the Conemaugh River near Johnstown, in the southwestern portion of the county. The Conemaugh River with its source in the Allegheny range flowed westerly toward Pittsburgh and into the Ohio country via the wide Ohio River. The Conemaugh River had been used by the local Indians, and later boatmen and hunters, as a liquid highway to the West for the last half century. They would build small rafts in Johnstown after crossing the mountain divide then float downstream. It was in Pittsburgh where Meriwether Lewis of the famous Lewis & Clark Expedition built their specially designed 55-foot keelboat, called the *Discovery*, for the trip down the Ohio River to St. Louis in August 1803.

Rowland Humphreys

Rowland Humphreys was living in Cambria County at this important period of transition from frontier to settled community. After his arrival in 1815, he resided in Ebensburg and worked as a merchant. Ebensburg was a small town of just 28 families — 168 people — in 1820.[1] Almost all of the in-town businesses were involved in some form of localized manufacturing like tin smith, leather works, candle maker, blacksmith and so on, to support the town's very existence. The town really did resemble a colony of some sorts. A few short years later, in 1818, Rowland married Catherine Mariner and started his family. Their first three children died in infancy, and it looked as if they were not going to ever have a family. In March 1823, the couple bought a house on Lot #53 in Ebensburg from Stephen Lloyd for $250. The house was located on the northeast corner of Sample and Julian Streets, a few blocks from the hustle and bustle of High Street where Rowland worked as a businessman and merchant. High Street, which ran east to west, is where the Indiana, Huntingdon, & Cambria Turnpike entered and exited the town on its way west to Indiana County. This new turnpike, built in 1820, greatly contributed to the area's physical and economic growth during the 1820s. The isolated Welsh colony was not so isolated anymore.

In April 1823, a son was born to the Humphreys whom they named John, after their first son who died in 1822. A succession of children followed: William was born in March 1825, David in 1827, and Mary in 1829. By 1830, they had four children and another one on the way. Thomas was born in early 1830, Hannah in 1832, James in 1835, and Ann in 1837. Rowland and Catherine had eleven children in fifteen years, seven of whom survived.

Salt

By 1833, High Street in Ebensburg had become the business center of the whole county. The turnpike, which ran directly through the town utilizing High Street, became a supply station for wagon trains heading west. Rowland was working as a butcher and salt merchant along High Street—a much coveted occupation, since salt-cured meat was needed by the emigrants for their westward trek. In July 1833, Rowland purchased 30 barrels of salt from a large salt mining operation in Saltsburg, where it was produced from boiling down large vats of saltwater brought up from underground wells. Rowland advertised his salt supply for six months, starting in July. The *Ebensburg Sky* reported: "JUST RECEIVED, and for sale by the barrel or bushel, 30 BARRELS SALT; which will be sold low and *Cash or County Produce*. Apply to the subscriber. R. HUMPHREYS. Ebensburg july [*sic*] 4, 1833."[2] Rowland's business included the three hundred or so local residents in Ebensburg, and the emigrants that rode by his store every day west at "the pace of a wagon." At this slow pace, it gave him plenty of time to rush out the front door of his shop and bark out at the drivers to "buy your salt now or regret it later." Unbeknown to the wagon trains of emigrants at the time, the salt sold to them was extracted west of Ebensburg along the route to Pittsburgh. They could have bought it in another day's travel. Nonetheless, there never seamed to be an end of emigrants ready to buy the much-needed salt.

In the summer of 1833, near Rowland's business on High Street, the principal office for the newly organized "Allegheny Portage Rail-Road" was established. Their job was to oversee the construction of the first railroad over the Allegheny Mountains on behalf of the Commonwealth of Pennsylvania to bring commerce east from the West. This new railroad and the canal basins were the biggest thing in the country since the building of the Erie Canal. This railroad, if successful, could bring in thousands of new people and hundreds of contract jobs to Ebensburg and Cambria County. Rowland's salt days and chasing wagons were just about over.

Chapter Two
The Allegheny Portage Railroad

The Idea of the Main Line

The idea of a Pennsylvania Main Line Canal System and the Allegheny Portage Rail-road was not just to link isolated Cambria County to the eastern half of Pennsylvania, but to enable Pennsylvania to participate in the western trade business. (The word "rail-road" was originally two words but was condensed to just "railroad" a few years after.) The much larger picture outside of Cambria County was painted by eastern businesses and ambitious politicians in New York, Pennsylvania, and Maryland. Pennsylvania wanted to secure a large share of the Midwest trade traffic that for decades had avoided the eastern divide. Almost all of the Midwest trade traffic used the Mississippi River water route instead of going up and over the mountains. The Mississippi trade route flowed south through the city of New Orleans, then out to the Gulf of Mexico and up the Atlantic coast to the northern markets. This trade route was over one hundred years old. The Mississippi River route avoided the state of Pennsylvania altogether. Unbelievable as it may sound, traffic from eastern Ohio and Pittsburgh—roughly only four hundred miles from Philadelphia—would take up to six weeks to travel the several thousand miles of the southern route. The Allegheny and Blue Ridge Mountains that for so long hemmed in the country, also were separating the new country from the wealth of the West.

The Two Canals

But the Mississippi River was just one-half of the equation of capturing the western trade routes. The other half was the

6

unbridled success of the newly built Erie Canal in upstate New York extending from Albany to Buffalo. The Erie Canal was one of the most ambitious canal projects ever built in the world and was truly an engineering marvel of the 19th century. Its intention was to serve as the first water route to link the West with the major eastern seaport of New York City. The Erie Canal extended from the Hudson River near Albany westward along the Mohawk Valley to Syracuse, then to the Great Lakes near Buffalo, a distance of 364 miles. Work on the canal began in 1818 and the canal opened in 1825. Upon completion, the Erie Canal used 84 locks and rose only 650 feet in elevation throughout its entire 364-mile length. The Erie Canal impacted all shipping patterns in America from 1825–1900.[1] Because of its construction, cargo could flow directly east to west, avoiding the southern Mississippi route entirely.

Maryland

Not to be outdone by New York, Maryland began to construct the Chesapeake & Ohio Canal in July 1828. Proposed to be completed in the 1830s, the C&O Canal closely followed the north shore of the Potomac River and linked Washington, D.C. (actually Georgetown) to the Ohio River near Wheeling, Virginia. The Chesapeake & Ohio Canal took longer to build and cost more than the Erie Canal because of winding curves, and mountains to cross. Add to this the advent of the Baltimore & Ohio Railroad in 1827, and Maryland appears to have been in possession of the nation's economic future. This was great news to the businessmen of Baltimore

Meanwhile, bankers in Philadelphia and politicians in Harrisburg saw things much differently and were fearful that lucrative trade to the West would be lost to either the Erie Canal or the Chesapeake & Ohio Canal. Added together, the two massive canal systems and the B&O RR could squeeze the commercial life out of the port city of Philadelphia and ultimately the Commonwealth of Pennsylvania. In March 1824, a three-member Board of Canal Commissioners was appointed by Governor John Schulze,

The canal basins on the Pennsylvania Main Line System of Canals looked and functioned the very same way as the C&O Canal's. Canal technology and construction methods were well known, but railroad technology in the late 1820s and early 1830s was an ongoing work. The C&O Canal National Historic Park.

Early rail-roads as they appeared in local newspapers. Horsepower was still the hoof.

consisting of Colonel Jacob Holgate, James Clark, and Charles Treziyulney, to develop a realistic economic strategy for the state.

Their plan—to build the state's very own canal system to compete against its neighbors—was not much different than that of New York and Maryland. They were going to build a rival canal system that was better, faster, and cheaper! This canal project was designed to link Philadelphia, along the Delaware River, to the capital Harrisburg, along the Susquehanna River, to Pittsburgh, along the Ohio River, and beyond. It would provide a shorter route for western freight coming up the Ohio River to Pittsburgh than going all the way to Buffalo along the Great Lakes and the Erie Canal.

By February 1826, a year after the Erie Canal was opened, the Pennsylvania Main Line Canal System was quickly approved, funded, and under construction. Like the Erie Canal to the north, it was one of the most ambitious canal projects ever built in the world and was truly one of the engineering marvels of the 19th century. The surveyed route would be four hundred miles long, from Philadelphia and the Delaware River all the way across the state to Pittsburgh where the Ohio River began. The survey for the Main Line chose Cambria County as the location of the mountain crossing. "Canals in the clouds" may have sounded dreamy and romantic, but it still had to be built. The proposed survey route was to cross right over the Summit of Allegheny Mountain.

The canal construction took several backbreaking years, cost millions of dollars, and involved thousands of men. But Pennsylvanians were just as energetic as their counterparts in New York and Maryland. There was no cure to "canal fever" in the 1820s. Every state had to have one.

If the whole Pennsylvania Main Line Canal System were successful, it would change the political, economical, social, and geographical landscape of the new frontier. If it worked as planned, Philadelphia would remain an important seaport for exports. If successful, Pittsburgh might become an important frontier river town someday—even become the "Gateway to the West." Smaller towns along the canal route between Philadelphia and Pittsburgh, like Hollidaysburg, Ebensburg, and Johnstown, could become important towns too someday. If on the other hand, the Main Line failed to work as planned, and not bring in the trade of the West, it would cost millions of dollars and quite a few political heads. But it had to be completed, and time was running out. It was too big and important a conquest for the state of Pennsylvania to ignore.

The Democrats and the Whigs

Because this project was so important to Pennsylvania and impacted the lives of a large number of citizens, approval and funding had to come at the state level. Federal money for such projects was unheard of. During the 1820s, it was more important to have strong political representation in your own state house than in Washington. This is where the power was; this is where important things got done. State needs, and even some local needs, were much more important than national needs, except during periods of war. After war time activities, states usually went back to their own unique state problems such as expanding their own ports and harbors or building turnpikes. For the most part, throughout the 1820s, the Democratic Party was a majority in the Pennsylvania state house, governor's office, and local county governments.[2] The Democrats were determined to get the approval and funding and complete the Main Line as soon as possible.

Ironically, this type of public works project was more to the liking of the minority political party — the Whigs. The Whig Party was a political party organized around the goals of promoting a national bank, high foreign tariffs, but most importantly, to promote public works projects in America for the good of the people.[3] In the 1820s it was the promotion of competing canals, later in the 1840s it was the promotion of competing railroads.

The Pennsylvania Democrats and their fellow Whigs both wanted the Main Line Canal System built. In 1825, the canal system was approved over the opposition of northern Pennsylvania counties who could see no tangible benefit of a canal system that did not involve them at all. Nonetheless, in the late 1820s, hundreds of miles of public canals were approved and financed by

Newspaper advertisement from the 1830s

the state, and built from Philadelphia to Pittsburgh. The building of the new canals and railroads would provide thousands of construction jobs, and long term jobs for their operation. Along with the state jobs came patronage, and along with the patronage came politics. Political patronage was needed to get things built like turnpikes and canals and the new railroads in the 1820s. Remote and distant Cambria County, the selected site for the mountain crossing of the Main Line Canal System, the place where the "canals would meet the clouds," would get its fair share of patronage too—if you were a Democrat.

The Pennsylvania Canal

In the beginning, a canal was proposed for the entire length from Philadelphia to Pittsburgh, similar to the Erie Canal connecting Albany to Buffalo with a single direct water route. However, problems such as traversing the western mountains in canal boats seem to disfavor that canal. New York did not have mountain crossing problems to deal with, so their canal was relatively easy to design and build in comparison to Pennsylvania's. At the same time, another idea was proposed: a railroad. A railroad route was considered for the entire four hundred-mile length through Pennsylvania by a few visionaries but was scoffed at by politicians as being "too new" and untested a technology for such an important project. There were also other problems associated with railroads, and they were treated much differently than canals:

At the time when railroads were introduced into this country, the plans for operating them entered largely into the discussions as to their superiority and usefulness. The weight of popular opinion was in favor of the rules governing turnpike roads and adverse to centering the control of motive power on them either in the agents of the Commonwealth, individuals, firms, or corporations. Monopoly was the bugbear in the dreams of the people, whilst the greatest good to the country was expected to follow giving to each and every individual citizen the largest liberty to roam as a carrier over the railroad at such times and in such a way as would suit his own convenience. It required actual performance to educate the people and demonstrate the fact that good results could only be obtained by intelligent administration and executive control of railroads being centered in a proper and absolute authority.[4]

The system proposed by the Canal Board was somewhat a hybrid of the two transportation systems, utilizing the best of both technologies in prime locations. Several canals and railroads would be linked together. The Pennsylvania Main Line Canal System would then be built in the following manner: First, a railroad of 81 miles between Philadelphia and Columbia, to be called the Columbia Railroad (one of the first railroads in America). Second, two canal basins, totaling a length of 173 miles from Columbia to Hollidaysburg, would be needed. The first canal started in Columbia, followed the Susquehanna River to Duncan's Island (near Harrisburg), and was called the Eastern Division. The second canal went from Duncan's Island to Hollidaysburg, followed the Juniata River, and was called the Juniata Division. The third canal, this one 104 miles long, followed the Conemaugh River from Johnstown to Pittsburgh on the western slope of the Alleghenies, and was called the Western Division. And finally, a 36-mile connector route between the Juniata and Western Canals was needed to complete the four hundred-mile route. What was needed to complete the system was a center or connecting piece over Allegheny Mountain. To finally link East to West! But how?

A canal, a roadway, or another new fangled railroad? Following is a report from the Board:

> In short, the whole country, from the upper forks of the Juniata to the forks of the South branch of the Conemaugh is mountainous; mountain rising after mountain in quick secession. The main one where the proposed tunnel is to pass, is hemmed in and surrounded by other high mountains, with steep slopes separated from one another by narrow ravines and presenting no favorable situation for canalling, either by lockage or tunneling. Here nature has refused to make her usual kind advances to aid the exertions of man; mountains are thrown together, as if to defy human ingenuity, and baffle the skill of the engineer.
>
> Charles Treziyulney, third Commissioner,
> Report to Governor,
> February 21, 1825[5]

The mountain portion was key in making the entire Main Line operate as designed. In 1825, if one was sitting in the office

The great barrier, the Allegheny Mountains, separates central from western Pennsylvania. The mountain rises more than 1,400 feet above Hollidaysburg in less than 10 horizontal miles. Sugar Run Gap, shown here, was one such mountain crossing to the West.

of the Canal Commissioners in Harrisburg, the small "hilly" portion on the state map between Hollidaysburg and Johnstown looked more like a minor inconvenience than a major hindrance. The hilly portion prevented the canals from going straight through from the Juniata to the Western Canal basin. Without this 36-mile portion completed, the entire canal line would end short of its destination of Pittsburgh. This meant failure. Funding for the entire project was approved by the state legislature in 1826, and the "green light" was given to begin the state-owned works with or without the mountain crossing decided upon. Nonetheless, construction on the canals started later that year. The problem had to wait.

In 1828, after two long years of construction on the Juniata Canal Division, the Allegheny Mountain range was within view of the canal workers, yet no decision had been reached regarding how to cross it. Initially, the canal system was going to be the only transportation system throughout the mountains, until engineers realistically addressed the "hilly portion" problem. The "hilly" problem was *very* real and *very* large—Allegheny Mountain rose 1,400 feet from the canal basin in Hollidaysburg to the Summit in a mere 10 horizontal miles. In addition to this dramatic elevation increase, it was also steeper on the Hollidaysburg side than the western side of the mountain. One suggested plan to cross the mountain was to utilize a canal-lock system to rise above the mountains and descend on the other side. This would provide a one hundred percent water highway from Columbia to Pittsburgh, with no breaks in changing the form of transportation—again, similar to the Erie Canal. A second suggested idea was to build a 36-mile turnpike over the mountain connecting each canal basin. This would have been the simplest of ideas. A third proposed idea was to construct an incline railroad. This railroad would be the most challenging of ideas. The final proposed idea was a system of canal locks along with a four and a-half mile canal tunnel through the mountain, at a cost of $480,000.[6] A tunnel of this size had never been attempted before. This hybrid solution was wisely voted down by the three canal commissioners, and a short connecting roadway was decided upon instead. But what type of roadway; rock or rail? Iron heels or iron wheels?

At this same time, the advancing technology of the railroad made it more practical every day. The first true railroad built in the U.S. was the Baltimore & Ohio RR in 1828 in Maryland, although it utilized only horses for power until 1830. The first locomotives were put into operation the following year, 1829, in Reading, Pennsylvania, on yet another railroad. Slowly, steam-powered locomotives were becoming stronger and larger every year after 1829 with the advent of technological changes and inventions. This railroad idea was looking very promising for the Main Line. Besides, the use of a turnpike over Allegheny Mountain would "require six to eight hours for stages and twelve to fourteen for wagons."[7] Perhaps a railroad could function as a speedy intermediate gap between the two canal divisions. One was already being built on the Main Line between Columbia and Philadelphia. Perhaps along with the newest and best canal system in the country, this mountain railroad would prove to be another shining star for the Keystone state. Engineers from all over the country would come to central and western Pennsylvania to gaze on an engineering wonder and delight in its daily operation. To add to the overall railroad excitement an overzealous mapmaker in Philadelphia by the name of Anthony Finley published a Pennsylvania state map with a "Rail Road" already connecting the south fork of the Little Conemaugh River near Johnstown up and over Allegheny Mountain into Bedford County, then to the little town of Newry in Huntingdon County. It was a bold map—almost a promotion. A year later, in 1830, the Western Canal Division of the Main Line System was completed to Johnstown where the link would begin. The canal commissioners had to make a decision about what to do about the dreaded mountain crossing. Time was running out. Money was becoming tight. By this point the three canals were nearly complete.

In 1830, the painful decision was finally made by the canal commissioners about the great mountain link of the Main Line System. An inclined railroad would be built. The idea of a railroad connecting the two western canal basins was finally accepted

Map of Cambria County, Pa., 1830

N

CAMBRIA COUNTY

INDIANA COUNTY

Loretto

Ebensburg

HUNTINGDON COUNTY

Munster

Hollidaysburg

Proposed 4-mile tunnel

Little Juniata River

Newry

Conemaugh River

(Gap)

Johnstown

1829 "Finley" Map

BEDFORD COUNTY

SOMERSET COUNTY

- Proposed RR Route

- Overland Turnpike

- Important Rivers

- Not to Scale

© Chris J. Lewie, 2001

and its eastern terminus would be at Hollidaysburg. The decision to choose Hollidaysburg over other nearby towns, like Newry, was by no means an accident. Hollidaysburg was where a good deal of the state's political power resided. Political power was necessary to get the project approved, funded, and underway. The railroad would link Johnstown to Hollidaysburg — and that was final!

The Main Line Cometh

By 1830, Rowland could have probably lived the rest of his life as a local businessman, parttime militia captain, father, in busy Ebensburg. But something happened on his road to genteel retirement. The Commonwealth of Pennsylvania declared that it was going to build a massive canal system from Philadelphia to Pittsburgh just a few miles away from his home. By 1830, practically everyone in America knew what a canal was and how it operated. But hardly anyone in America knew what a railroad was. Hardly anyone west of the Alleghenies had ever seen one in operation. This was going to be the farthest west one had ever been built.

Actually, the steam locomotive defined the industrial age since it was science in action. Railroads, locomotives, and steam power represented a "can-do" attitude by 1830. A future railroad was the talk of the town and helped start some as well. It was something that the community just had to have, or another community would build one first. Cambria County, whose population had more than doubled from 1820 to 1830, from 3,000 people to over 7,000 people, was not going to let this opportunity pass.

During the early 1830s anyone who lived close to a railroad was in one way or another affected by it. Farmers, bankers, stockbrokers, businessmen, laborers, and coal miners saw their way of life change. Business fortunes were quickly won and some lost on the rails. Political leaders strained to convey the railroad's importance to voters in local and state elections. Social ladders of the rich and famous were changed over night by this little steam invention. Others saw it differently altogether. Some saw it as the work of the devil in the form of an iron dragon; and did not even spare the railroad in their Sunday preachings. What they really saw was uncertainty. New technology had the tendency to do that. The Allegheny Portage Railroad would change the lives, fortunes, and status of families in Pennsylvania, including the Humphreys in Ebensburg.

By 1833, Rowland Humphreys moved to seize a new business opportunity as a railroad contractor. He had visited their main office in town, read the printed literature, looked at the surveys and maps, listened to flowery speeches, followed the construction activities in the newspapers, and decided that this was the future path for him and his family to follow.

The Needed Gap

The surveyed location of the ascending route of the railroad of the Allegheny Mountain was by no means an accident. It appeared simple on paper and quite natural within the lay of the land — follow the watersheds and upper forks backwards to their initial source; this would keep the grades down and elevations to less than 10 percent. Blairs Gap Run west of Hollidaysburg

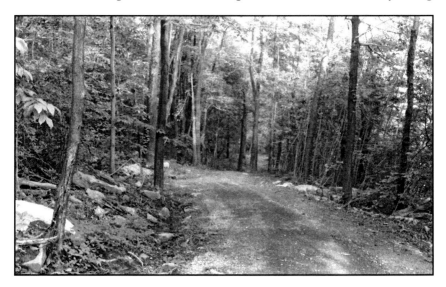

Roads in and out of eastern Cambria County in the early 1800s were no more than converted Indian trails, barely wide enough for wagons or stagecoaches. Canals through here would have been impossible.

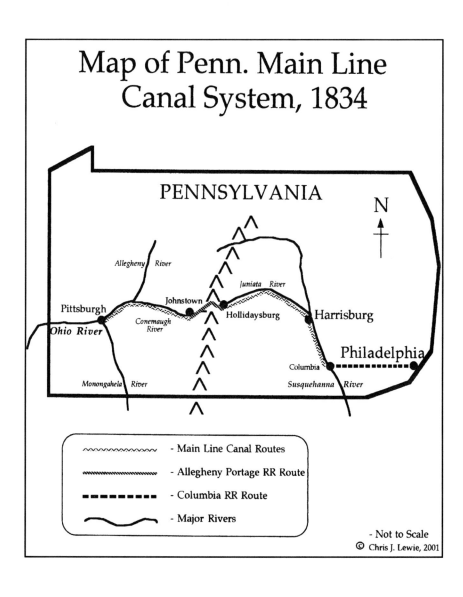

and the Juniata canal terminus found this plan most ideal. Hollidaysburg was located at the upper reach of the Juniata River basin just before the mountains. The existing turnpike was also located there and had resolved the problem of access over the mountain in 1820. The turnpike could also be utilized for hauling construction material, supplies, and men to and from the railroad work site without much difficulty. This was a huge cost savings to the Commonwealth.

The approved railroad route would begin in the town of Hollidaysburg. The route paralleled the existing dirt and gravel turnpike near the Bedford County line, passed Gallitzin Springs, and continued all the way to the Summit of the mountain. The new rail route would crisscross the existing turnpike only three times on its way to Johnstown; the first time near the base of the mountain and the second time near the top at the "Skew Arch" for the turnpike traffic to travel over and the railroad to cross under. Just past the Summit of the mountain, the rail route would cross the turnpike for the last time, then followed the Little Conemaugh River from its upper forks to Johnstown about 26 miles to the west. From Johnstown, the Western Canal route would take over from the mountain railroad and pass right through the 1,350-foot Conemaugh Gap of Laurel Ridge and on toward Pittsburgh. (The gap was the deepest gorge east of the Mississippi River.) Although the plans of the railroad were resolved in 1831, the right-of-way still had to be obtained, and the massive old growth trees needed to be cleared. Thousands of tons of stone and dirt had to be moved. The railroad itself still had to be built, as well as the 10 stationary engine houses. Each engine house had two steam engines, making 20 handmade steam engines in all. All of this had to come together before the first barrel of flour from Ohio could be brought back to Philadelphia.

In April 1831, Sylvester Welsh was appointed chief engineer of the project. He established the railroad office in Ebensburg along High Street and solicited contracts for its construction. Mr. Welsh had his work cut out for him. The entire Pennsylvania Main Line System and millions of dollars were banking on this little stretch of railroad to work. It had to. This was the center piece of the entire endeavor. A great deal of money and state pride were riding on it. New York and Maryland were already ahead of them in the canal game and time was running out.

The Engineering Problems

In late 1832, the Juniata Canal project was finished, and construction on the Portage Railroad had yet to begin. The construction of the railroad would be a massive undertaking and require countless surveys. Clearing a swath through the forest 120 feet wide for 36 miles, the building of 68 culverts and several bridges, and construction of the roadway and rail bed would take an additional year and the teamwork of two thousand freemen to complete. No slaves worked on the project. This was Pennsylvania — not Virginia. Even if the railroad were able to be constructed in just two years by freemen, several very real engineering problems existed. First, there were practically no railroad engineers in Pennsylvania, or America, at that time. The technology was too new for any formal training to be obtained in the United States. The best engineering school in America at that time was the US Military Academy at West Point, and they were primarily concerned with cartography, battlefield engineering and logistics, not railroad construction. That was looked upon by instructors there as bizarre and wasteful civilian activity. Most of the civil engineers of the time had been educated mainly in topographical engineering and trained in road and bridge building. Second, operating any steam engine system or boiler was dangerous in 1832, let alone one on wheels creeping up and down a steep, slippery mountain. Many steam engines of that time exploded due to being overstoked and a lack of general mechanical engineering knowledge to prevent such deadly accidents. The locomotives had to be designed and built to withstand everyday stresses such as pulling 20,000 pounds or climbing up fairly steep grades of five percent or more. The stationary engines, which were affixed to 10 locations and protected from the elements, were safer but had heavier loads to pull. Third, there were practically no canal engineers in America to merge these two transportation systems together at the railroad terminus, now called depots. The how-tos for the cargo and passenger transfers at the depots had to be worked out. Some canals and railroads were designed and built as working experiments in some places to resolve such everyday problems. Lawyers worked as construction engineers at times due to their education and ability to read technical drawings. So, to merge the two motive power systems together into one was going to be guesswork of the self-taught, self-ordained engineers of the day. Chief Engineer Sylvester Welsh had his hands full before the first engine was stoked and fired up.

In addition to this growing list of real-world engineering problems, a railroad tunnel and a bridge were needed near Johnstown to avoid additional track mileage and overall cost. A railroad tunnel had never been built before in America. This one was not going to be short. The Staple Bend Tunnel, as it was called, would be 901 feet long, 20 feet wide, and 19 feet high. But it had to be built in order to save on overall track length and cost of going around a bend in the Conemaugh River. So, plans on how this was going to be accomplished were drawn up too. Another engineering project was a bridge called the Conemaugh Viaduct. It was built four miles east of the tunnel to cross over the Conemaugh River. The viaduct had a 80-foot span and was nearly $78^1/_2$ feet high and, like the Staple Bend Tunnel, was quite an engineering achievement for its day. (The viaduct survived the Portage days only to be destroyed in the devastating Johnstown flood of May 31, 1889.) The technology to construct both tunnels and bridges was available but never applied to a railroad and its needs until that time. Just another problem that had to be resolved, and fast.

These construction problems could only be resolved by using manpower, horsepower, hand tools, and tons of black powder. The industrial age was about to commence, but construction of it had not. Brute force was needed. Shovels, picks, hammers, axes, chisels, crowbars, horse-drawn wagons, and black powder were the main components of heavy construction in 1830. Powered construction machinery such as steam shovels and drills was more than half a century away. The entire railroad had to be built through crude muscle power of men with no real professional engineering plans laid out before them. The self-taught canal and railroad engineers and contract laborers had their work cut out for them on this monster project.

The Railroad Name

The name chosen for the railroad in the early 1830s was the "Allegheny Portage Railroad." That name pretty well tells it all. Portage is both a noun and a verb. As a noun, *portage* refers to "the carrying of boats and goods overland between navigable bodies of water." As a verb, *portage* means "to carry gear over a portage." Both the noun and verb definitions fit appropriately. The Allegheny Mountain range provided the rest of the overall name, resulting in the "Allegheny Portage Railroad." For the most part, the Allegheny Portage Railroad was simply called "the Portage" by those that worked on it.

The Inclines and Planes

Mechanically speaking, the Portage was not a true railroad, but a series of inclines (often called "Planes") that utilized stationary engines to pull rail cars up and over the mountains at different stations. The 10 different engine houses (five on both sides of the Allegheny) were created to transfer the different rail cars between the inclines as they were hoisted up both directions east and west, where the going was more difficult or steep. Where it was not as steep (less than a one-percent grade), the rail cars were pulled by horses to the next incline, along an area called a level. This process, changing from inclines to levels and back again, was repeated until the entire 36-mile trip was completed at either the Johnstown or Hollidaysburg Depot. The Portage had 10 inclines and 11 levels, and the trip would take a good part of a day to complete. At the head of each incline was an engine house where two stationary engines of about 35 horse-power each moved the endless ropes attached to the cars. Two cars, loaded with 6,500 to 7,000 pounds each, were drawn up at once and could be let down at the same time; this operation could be performed from six to ten times in one hour. One stationary engine was used at any given time, with the other engine serving as a backup in

Wooden rails could be cut and shaped to conform with the contours of the land. The ongoing maintenance of the line presented a huge cost to the Commonwealth. Here the display by the National Historic Site shows a change in slope from Incline No. 6 to the engine house.

case of delays or the breakdown of the first stationary engine. It was also on standby in case the first broke down altogether.[8] This back-up plan, although wise, doubled the total cost of the engines.

The Route

The highest point of the Portage was 2,334 feet above sea level at the Summit of the mountain near Plane No. 6. The lowest point of the route was 946 feet above sea level at the depot in Hollidaysburg. This meant that the rise from Hollidaysburg to Summit was 1,388 feet in just 10 miles, with an average grade of 2.6 percent. However, it was the steepest portion of the rail route with grades averaging 8.86 percent on the eastern five planes. In the Johnstown area, the terminus was 26 miles or two and one-half times the distance from the Summit as Hollidaysburg, and dropped only 1,158 feet. The grades on the western slope averaged 8.36 percent on the five western planes, very similar to the eastern five planes of 8.86 percent, but the average grade

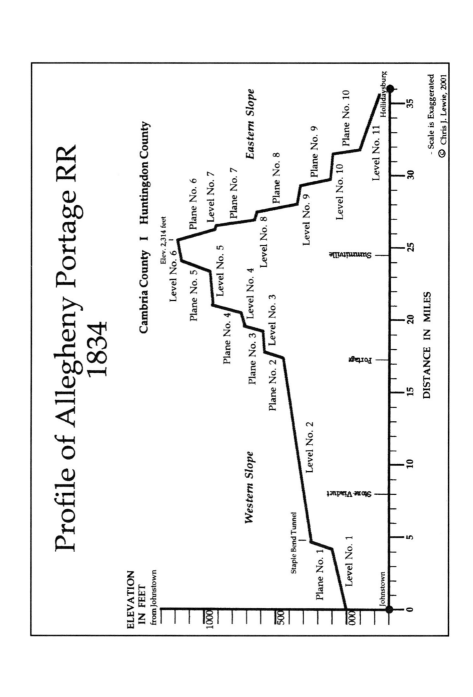

Profile of Allegheny Portage RR
1834

ELEVATION IN FEET from Johnstown

Cambria County **I** Huntingdon County

Western Slope

Eastern Slope

Staple Bend Tunnel

Plane No. 1
Level No. 1
Level No. 2
Plane No. 2
Level No. 3
Plane No. 3
Level No. 4
Plane No. 4
Level No. 5
Plane No. 5
Level No. 6
Elev. 2,314 feet
Plane No. 6
Level No. 7
Plane No. 7
Level No. 8
Plane No. 8
Level No. 9
Plane No. 9
Level No. 10
Plane No. 10
Level No. 11

Johnstown
Stone Viaduct
Portage
Summitville
Hollidaysburg

1000
500
000

DISTANCE IN MILES

0   5   10   15   20   25   30   35

- Scale is Exaggerated

© Chris J. Lewie, 2001

Incline Plane No. 6 as it descends into Blairs Run Gap toward Hollidaysburg. This fine display at the APRR National Historic Site shows how steep the slope actually was — a 9.70 percent grade. Note the Skew Arch Bridge at the bottom of the incline.

Thousands of stone blocks called "sleepers" were used to support the railroad along the 36-mile route. Each sleeper, about two feet by two feet by one foot, and weighing up to 60 pounds was quarried out of local sandstone found nearby. Sleepers can still be found today in the area.

The stone sleepers did have the tendency to move or shift after the winter's thaw in spring. Whole sections of rail lines would appear to slide down the hill in steeper locations. Additional ballast helped in some areas. The ballast surrounding the sleepers and rails was also from the locally quarried material used to make the sleepers, stone for buildings, and gravel lanes.

The Indiana, Huntingdon & Cambria Turnpike was finished in 1820 and is known today as old U.S. Rt. 22. This photo, taken in June 2000, shows the top of Blairs Gap Run near the summit of Allegheny Mountain.

Construction of the 36-mile Allegheny Portage Railroad required the removal of thousands of trees and thousands of tons of rock. A path 120 feet wide was created to keep tall trees from falling onto the tracks. Construction was by hand using axes, saws, picks, shovels, and tons of black powder.

for the 26-mile western route was less than one percent with longer levels, too. One level, No. 2, was over 13 miles long, and represented one-third of the entire railroad length. (See Profile on page 26.)

Cost

Engineer Moncure Robinson proposed the initial construction cost of just the Portage RR in 1829 was $936,004.87. This cost included a one-mile-long tunnel at the Summit to reduce overall track mileage of climbing and descending the crest.[9] The unpopular idea of the one-mile tunnel at the Summit was scratched, but a shorter one along the Stable Bend of the Conemaugh was approved by Governor Wolf by "An act to continue the improvement of the State by canal and railroads."[10] It was really needed there to reduce total length and save transportation time. The Staple Bend Tunnel cost $37,500, while the Conemaugh viaduct cost $55,000 to build.[11] Combined the two projects represented almost 10 percent of the entire railroad expense.

Conemaugh Viaduct

Roberts, *Reminiscences of the First Railroad over the Allegheny Mountain*

Construction of the Portage RR lasted from 1831 to late 1833. The railroad project was one of the largest of its kind under construction in America. It employed some two thousand men at one time. In November 1833, the 36-mile system was completed and test runs of railcars proved successful. But it was too late in the year to start up the whole railroad because winter was just a month away. In the following spring, March 1834, the single-track railroad from Hollidaysburg to Johnstown was ready for operation. The final cost of construction was $1.27 million (other quotes state $1.63 million[12] and even $1.83 million).[13] The total cost of the canals was $8.32 million and the Columbia RR's a whopping $4.2 million. The total construction cost of the Pennsylvania Main Line System from Philadelphia to Pittsburgh was $14.36 million. It was a hefty price to pay to be in the western trade business.

Rope

One of the last functions before the new railroad was operational was to haul the ropes to each of the 10 incline planes. The total length of the Russian hemp ropes for all the inclines was 50,347 feet and they weighed 18,649 pounds — when dry. In 1834, salt dealer Rowland Humphreys was contracted "...to re-distribute the ropes to each inclined plane" by wagons as soon as the weather permitted in the spring(s), for which he was paid $30.00, representing $3.00 or $3.50 per day, from the Rigger's Loft near Summitville to the various planes along the route, from Blairsville to the east to Johnstown in the west.[14] It would take Rowland several wagons and several days just to move the nearly 10 miles of coiled ropes to the various inclines from the Summit loft. The ropes were even heavier when wet after a spring shower and even more difficult to redistribute into position. Some ropes were segmented and woven into long sections, then spliced together on site at each engine house.[15]

The Grand Opening

After the ropes were in place and the engines fired up, the railroad opened for business at the Summit with great fanfare on March 18, 1834. It was a grand day for the Democrats as well as

The Skew Arch Bridge as it looked at about 1900.

The Skew Arch Bridge was built in 1832–33 to allow the turnpike to cross over the railroad without disrupting the flow of traffic for either. The stone bridge carried both horse and later automobile traffic for over one hundred years. The bridge is still standing today next to the old U.S. Rt. 22 (photo taken in 2000).

The Skew Arch Bridge is retired and no longer carries traffic but still is a reminder of the earlier industrial and transportation days of America.

The Lemon House was an important hotel along the turnpike near the Summit. The stone structure has been restored and is now protected by the National Park Service at the Allegheny Portage RR National Historic Site.

for the Commonwealth, and the residents of Cambria County. There were celebrations all along the entire route from Philadelphia to Pittsburgh. A reception was even held at the new Summit Hotel built at the crossroads of the turnpike and the railroad at the Summit of the mountain. Speeches were made, toasts were given, cannons were fired, and everyone was filled with excitement as the Pennsylvania Main Line was finally complete. By the time of the railroad's opening the Main Line canals had been operating for two years, as had the Columbia & Philadelphia Railroad. Everyone was waiting for this moment to assure linking the systems together. The Portage was finally finished and the entire system was ready for operation. The state-sponsored transportation system, dreamed up in 1826, was complete and ready to use. In the spring of 1834, a trip from Philadelphia to Pittsburgh by canal and rail now took only four and one-half days instead of the weeks' travel in 1830. This remarkable accomplishment in engineering and construction was great news for businessmen and travelers throughout the state, but there were now real problems — like running a mountain railroad.

Chapter Three
The Operation of the Portage

By March 1834, the transportation dream of the Commonwealth was a reality. The railroad was built. But now someone had to run and administer it. Solomon Roberts was hired as one of the first people to help survey, build, and run the railroad. He had this to say about the first year of operation in 1834:

> The experiment of working the road as a public highway was very unsatisfactory. Individuals and firms employed their own drivers, with their own horse and cars. The cars were small, had four wheels, and each car would carry about 7,000 lbs. of freight. Usually four cars made a train, and that number could be taken up, and as many let down, an inclined plane at one time, and from six to ten such trips could be made in an hour. The drivers were rough set of fellows, and sometimes very stubborn and unmanageable. It was not practicable to make them work by a time-table, and the officers of the railroad had no power to discharge them. My memory recalls the case of one fellow, who could not go backward, and could not go forward, and so obstructed the road for a considerable time. It resembled the case of two wild wagoners of the Alleghenies, meeting in a narrow mountain pass, and both refusing to give way. Our nominal remedy was to have the man arrested, and taken before a magistrate, perhaps many miles off, to have him fined according to the law, a copy of which I used to carry in my pocket.[1]

In the first full season the Portage carried 25,000 passengers, 15,437 westbound, and 9,563 eastbound, and carried 52,719 tons of freight; 29,740 tons westbound, 15,439 tons eastbound, and 7,540 tons locally.[2] Although the numbers were not quite showing an easterly majority of traffic, it was promising nonetheless. The second year would be much better, after some of the bugs were worked out.

Portage Men

By 1835, a second track had been laid, to avoid dreaded delays by independent minded hauling contractors, as Roberts describes. The second tract also enabled the development of a new counterbalance system to raise and lower the cars more efficiently. In 1835, just a few locomotives were in use between the inclines on the western slopes/levels so that most of the train's crews worked in a stationary engine house. Each of the initial 10 stationary engines were occupied by a crew that included an engineer, assistant engineer, a fireman, car tender (hitcher), and some laborers. All had to work together as a team in order for the entire railroad to operate efficiently.

The engineers had to operate, maintain the steam engine, and oversee almost every activity around them. The engineers would later operate the steam locomotives as they arrived after construction. It appears that a great deal of the engineer jobs on the Portage were given out locally to those who could read and write, had some common mechanical sense, and were involved in the Democratic Party. Again, patronage was in full bloom. No jobs were "imported" for this aspect of the operation. The engineers' job was to insure that the engines were in fine working condition, nothing exploded, and the mail, people, and freight got to their destination in one piece. They also had to make sure that they did not overload the boilers and kill themselves (or unsuspecting passengers) in the event of an explosion. Courage was perhaps the most necessary element to operate the steam engines. The work was dangerous, noisy, and gritty, but very exciting. Needless to say, the engineer had the choice of jobs, and better pay, but most of all a newfound status in the community — one of awe. Two engineers were usually located at each incline

Next to the Lemon House is the recreated Engine House No. 6, where the Humphreys worked as engineers in the 1840s. This engine house and Plane No. 6 are part of the APRR National Historic Site.

Inside the engine house are the 35-horsepower steam engines and general operating mechanics. The cut-away display shows the wheels, pulleys, and hemp rope that pulled the cars up the mountain.

shed—the other being an assistant engineer. When the Portage opened in 1835, engineers made between $1.37½ and $2.00 per day.[3] Back then these were decent wages, but during the next 20 years the wages rarely increased. In later years, engineers were given a company house complete with fuel for heating as compensation for their duties, and other perks. The wages, over the period, were as follows: engineers of stationary engines, $1.50 to $1.68¾ per day; assistant engineers of stationary engines, $1.00 to $1.25 per day; firemen of stationary engines, $0.87½ per day; and car tender, $0.75 per day.[4]

The firemen maintained the fires and boilers at a constant temperature and fed the 60 bushels of coal into the open furnace, daily. This was a never-ending process of shoveling and stoking the boilers for up to 12 hours a day, 276 days a year—a hot, sweaty job, especially in the summer when the outside temperatures were in the 90s and the inside temperatures well over 100 degrees. Due to the constant shoveling, firemen were lean and sleek in appearance.

The car tenders (or hitchers) did just that—they hitched cars to both the incline rope and the locomotives. They also checked the ropes and rails for wear and tear. It was a very dangerous job that sometimes cost fingers or toes during the hitching process. A good tender was one that had all 10 of his fingers and all 10 of his toes at the end of each season. Besides the ropes, runaway cars would come crashing down from up hill, causing a great deal of damage and even death at the bottom. Tenders had to be attentive at all times. Their lives depended on it. Some less enthusiastic travelers chose to walk alongside the moving railcars instead of inside for fear that the ropes would break (quite often they did), and they would be hurt or even killed in the mayhem that took place. Later a "train captain" was assigned to the locomotive train as an extra guiding member—a forerunner of modern train conductors and flagmen. Brakemen also were added for safety. The employment of those additional men cut down on car damage, injuries, and deaths considerably. But it was still extremely dangerous!

The laborers did everything else such as fetch the cordwood, coal, clean the tracks of fallen debris, tend the horses, shovel the horse manure, and clean out the fire pits and boilers, and dump the cold cinders. They kept stray livestock and people (especially unattended children and imbeciles) off the tracks and fetched the never-ending buckets of water for the boilers, if pipes from a nearby stream were not utilized. They also loaded and unloaded the cars from the canal boats and delivered daily messages up and down the mountain. Laborers sometimes doubled as flagmen during bad weather and when visibility was low, which was often. The flagmen signaled coded messages back and forth to the next engine houses, when the houses were visible.

Other employees such as blacksmiths, carpenters, boatmen, drivers, haulers, blowers, and strikers, and lots of common laborers were involved with the railroad. There were, of course, the ever-working maintenance crews of a dozen men who repaired portions of the railroad almost daily. Riggers strung the long hemp ropes to and from each plane in the spring and stored them in December at the end of the rail season.

Everyone employed by the railroad was instilled with the duty of getting the cargo and passengers over the dangerous mountains from Hollidaysburg to Johnstown, or vice versa, in one piece without any damage. Safety had a different meaning than it does today. Minor accidents occurred daily. Losing a finger or a toe was not as bad as losing an arm or a leg. Fatalities to workers and travelers occurred yearly regardless of attentiveness. Sometimes it was just a matter of luck and fate. Danger was everywhere on the Portage. It was a part of everyday life.

According to payroll sheets in 1839, the railroad operated every day for 12 hours, every day of the week, even Sunday, the Christian Sabbath. Traffic counts on Sunday were only 10 percent of that of a normal workday.[5] This reduced traffic might explain why the horses used to haul cars on the levels usually got one day off a week to rest—Sundays. But the men did not. Employees rarely took a day off, working 90 out of 91 days during a three-month stretch, and in some instances even on Independence

Day. Horses were at times treated better, and their owners were paid the same or even more than the men.

The Locomotives

In 1835, the first real locomotives, "Boston," "Delaware," and "Allegheny," were put into use on the Portage rail line to speed up things. The self-propelled locomotives, unlike the stationary railroad, turned the Portage into a real mobile rail-road. The locomotives were used mainly on the long levels on the western slope of the mountain between Johnstown and the Summit. By today's standards, the locomotives were extremely small, only $8^1/_2$ to 10 tons, inefficient, dirty, dangerous, and noisy.[6] The locomotives were custom-made by blacksmiths, metal workers, and mechanics. They had two large driving wheels in the back and two small guiding wheels in the front and rode on rails 4 feet $8^1/_2$ inches apart. They burned wood and belched clouds of black smoke and hot cinders behind them. They also were installed with a signal bell and a high-pitch steam whistle that could be heard by everyone nearby in the case of a collision. These types of locomotives generated only a small amount of horsepower and could haul only two to three cars plus a tender. The first locomotives had open air cabs and exposed the engineers to all the elements. Most of the early engineers wore a heavy wool or even leather full-length coat to protect them from the weather, the soot, and hot cinders. Slowly but surely, more complex and powerful locomotives were added to the Portage line in the following few years.

Rowland Humphreys did not jump on the opportunity to become one of the first engineers on these locomotives as others did. That was a job for the younger guys who were single, daring, and energetic. According to some people in Ebensburg they were just plain stupid to risk their lives on such an unproven and dangerous contraption. But that did not stop them from trying. Some folks opted to become contractors for the railroad. Some provided horsepower to move the cars between the inclines, and at the two depots. Other contractors provided the much-needed

A replica of the "Lafayette" steam locomotive on display at the APRR National Historic Site, near Gallitzin. This Norris design was common in the 1830s and 1840s and weighed about 10 tons.

cords of firewood and bushels of coal for the hungry boilers and steam engines. Still others provided general equipment and hardware to the system such as shovels, picks, chisels, candles, rope, and other items. Most contractors appeared to be local merchants and businessmen along the Portage route in Cambria and Huntingdon (later Blair) County. As a whole, they provided the majority of either goods or services used by the Portage.

During 1835, 50,000 tons of freight and 20,000 passengers were carried over the mountain.[7] Things were now picking up steam as the operation of the system became better and better. Before the close of the year 1835 all the work on the road had been completed with the exception of the depots and machine shops at Hollidaysburg and Johnstown. The Board of Canal Commissioners, in their report under date of December 2, 1835, submitted through Governor Wolf to the legislature, felicitated that body in the following language: "After nine years of unremitted toil and untiring perseverance in the construction and completion

Early locomotives as they appeared in local newspapers and business ledgers.

of upwards of six hundred miles of canal and slackwater navigation and nearly one hundred and twenty miles of railroads, Pennsylvania has placed herself on an eminence from whence she may
view without any apprehension of successful revelry the emulous
exertions of her sister States in similar enterprises."[8]

The next year, 1836, about 30,000 cars passed over the route.
This was 5,000 more than in 1835. *The Canal and Portage Register*
reported on July 27, 1836: "The business done on the line at
present, considering the season of the year, is far beyond what
was anticipated by even men who are concerned in the different
lines. The pack-et boats that arrive and leave this place daily, are
generally filled with passengers."[9] Even with all of the inherent
problems such as steep inclines, cutting through virgin forest,
wet conditions, lack of existing railroads, and winter thaws, it
looked like the railroad was going to work as designed after all.

By 1837, the fourth season of operation, 12 locomotives were
in use. By 1839, there were 17 locomotives. The "Allegheny," the
namesake of the railroad, cost $5,500, and the "Boston" $6,997 to
build. The other locomotives had names like the "Backwoodsman,"
"United States," and the "Constitution." More patriotic names were
used like the "George Washington," the "Benjamin Franklin," the
"Robert Morris," the "James Madison," and "Lafayette." They were
made by builders like William Norris, E. A. G. Young, and McClurg,
Wade & Co. "These machines were all doing fairly well, but the
Norris make excelled all others, doing double the amount of work,
with half the quantity of oil and fuel, and not requiring half the
amount of repairs."[10]

The Canal Men

The canal men or "Canallers," as they were called, were some
of the roughest and toughest men of their day. The work on the
canals lasted all day even during some of the worst possible
weather. The difficult conditions required good pay and attracted
all types of men—some less desirable than others. It was often
said that canal men were stubborn because of their rough attitude that sometimes created problems with freight movement
before anything could reach the Portage. Therefore the state

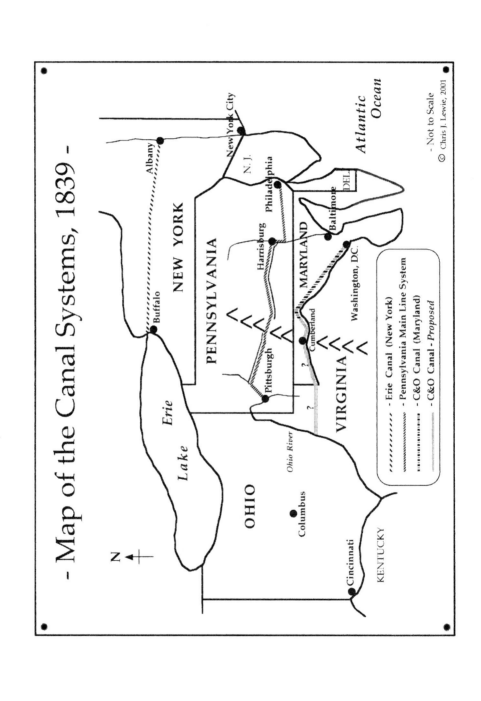

- Map of the Canal Systems, 1839 -

Lake Erie

Atlantic Ocean

N

OHIO

Columbus

Cincinnati

KENTUCKY

Ohio River

NEW YORK

Buffalo

Albany

New York City

N.J.

PENNSYLVANIA

Pittsburgh

Harrisburg

Philadelphia

DEL.

MARYLAND

Baltimore

Washington, DC.

Cumberland

VIRGINIA

- Not to Scale

© Chris J. Lewie, 2001

- Erie Canal (New York)
- Pennsylvania Main Line System
- C&O Canal (Maryland)
- C&O Canal - *Proposed*

needed to enforce certain regulations on them to create a better image of the Main Line System. The following is a circular posted by the Main Line Canal Board of Commissioners in February 1842 underscoring the need for "good, honest, and sober individuals" to work on the canals. It was that important:

CIRCULAR
TO SUPERVISORS AND COLLECTORS,

CANAL COMMISSIONERS' ROOM,
HARRISBURG, FEBRUARY 7, 1842.

SIR:

As it is very desirable the several lines of Canal in Pennsylvania be opened for navigation as early as practicable in the Spring, your attention is particularly directed to the accomplishment of this object. You will make all necessary repairs on your division as speedily as possible.

In the appointment of FOREMEN on your division, you will have particular reference to the public interest, and the economy of expenditure; and it is believed that not less than ten, nor more than fifteen miles of Canal should be allotted to one Foreman. The shortest division should be where the Canal is most liable to injury; and as it is of the utmost importance for the public service that the Agents of the Government should be honest, active, sober and industrious men, we trust that none but such will be employed by you.

The LOCK KEEPERS on your division should be capable, sober and attentive men, and none but such should hold these situations. A neglect of duty on their part, will be sufficient cause for their dismissal.

It has been represented to the Board that Collectors of Toll have exchanged current money for that which is less so. Any Collector who may be guilty of such conduct in future, will be regarded as offending against the express directions of this Board, and such offense will be inexcusable.

Whenever the use of a flat can be dispensed with upon your line, let it be done.

The utmost vigilance is enjoined upon you in the Supervision of your division, as well as the most rigid economy in your disbursements, and punctuality in the settlement of your accounts; and the use of public money in your hands for any other purpose than the service of the Commonwealth in the performance of your duties, is positively prohibited.

A copy of this Circular is also forwarded to each of the Collectors of Toll. From them a punctual settlement of their accounts, and a rigid accountability is required. They are absolutely prohibited from using the public money for private purposes, and wherever it is ascertained that the money of the Commonwealth is wrongfully used, it will be deemed a sufficient cause for immediate removal.

(*By order of the Board.*)

THOMAS L. WILSON,
Secretary.[11]

Canal Boats

Canal boats were most important to the canal basins where they transported passengers and freight, but not to the overall

A model of a sectional canal boat on a flatbed car at the APRR National Historic Site. Although famous for the idea of "canal boats in the clouds," the Portage really carried a very small percentage of canal boats in comparison to overall cars moved in any given year.

Another canal boat and rail car model on display at the National Historic Site. Earlier locomotives could pull only a few cars due to their limited horsepower and the extreme mountain conditions.

A simple friction brake called a "buck" was used behind the last rail car and saved a great deal of lives and cargo. A runaway car would ride upon the braking truck and press down on its wheels, slowing it down and even stopping it before disaster struck. The word "buck" may have been combined from the two words "braking truck." Model on display at the APRR National Historic Site.

success of the Portage Railroad. The boats came in all shapes and sizes but basically had a four-foot draft and could hold several tons of cargo. Segmented canal boats were introduced on the Portage in October 1834, by John Doughtery of the Reliance Transportation Line, but never really caught on in great numbers. Records indicate that even when flatbed rail cars were specifically designed to haul canal boats up and over the mountain they only represented a small portion of the overall traffic and weight on the Portage. For example, in 1849, one of the most successful years of the Portage, they represented only 4.3 percent of all tonnage traffic.[12] Canal boats not taken over the route intact were unloaded at the basin, their cargo reloaded on rail cars at the depot, taken over, and reloaded onto another canal boat in the next basin. Although this method of loading, unloading, and reloading was necessary for the movement of cargo during the 1830s, it became costly by the 1850s. After 1854, after twenty years' usage, canal boats on rail cars were no longer part of the Portage RR.

Rail Traffic and Passengers

The Portage RR and the Main Line canals were a boon to the local economy of Cambria, Huntingdon, and Allegheny Counties. Tens of thousands of dollars in goods flowed back and forth over the mountains every day, and hundreds of people, if not thousands, were involved in the railroad's use in one way or another. This included the railroad employees, canal workers, lock masters, local merchants, salesmen, farmers, lumbermen, and coal miners, to name a few. Some cargoes had local destinations such as Duncansville, Hollidaysburg, or Johnstown, while others traveled long distances to Philadelphia, Pittsburgh, Cincinnati, Ohio, or even St. Louis, Missouri. Shortly after the opening of the railroad, a turnpike connection was constructed between Ebensburg and Jefferson (Wilmore), which was located on the Portage RR line. The road was designed to connect the overland turnpike that flowed through Ebensburg to the railroad and the canals in Johnstown. Traffic was designed to flow downhill from Ebensburg to the rail line in Jefferson. Even though the Portage Railroad was slow, only 10-15 miles per hour, compared to the alternative of a mountain turnpike, it moved cargo and people much faster than a team of horses ever could for that distance and terrain. When it opened in 1834, the railroad charged a tonnage tax of five mills per ton-mile, per its charter. This was later reduced to three mills per ton for better competition. The railroad had its hierarchy of importance:

> In operating the road, trains drawn by locomotive en-
> gines were given the preference over horses and the descrip-
> tion of traffic hauled had preference in the following order:
> First, United States mails; second, passengers; third, burdens.
> ...Those drawing cars containing the United States mails and
> passengers were allowed to move at a rate of speed not ex-
> ceeding 15 miles, and those drawing burden cars not exceed-
> ing 10 miles per hour, except when passing bridges or over
> viaducts...[13]

Trains were slowly starting to fall into regular schedules for better service and to insure the public of some sort of daily routine:

> Everyday there was was one regular passenger train each
> way. It was a daylight railroad, never running any trains at
> night.[14] When sunset appeared the freight trains stopped at
> the first place until the sun rose again the next morning. The
> passenger train usually left Johnstown between 6 and 7
> o'clock in the morning, on the arrival of the packet from the
> west, and ran to Plane No. 2, (where the favorite hotels were),
> for breakfast, arriving at Hollidaysburg between 1 and 2
> o'clock. The west-bound train left about the same hour and
> arrived at Johnstown before 2 o'clock.
>
> A passenger train, in the latter days, consisted of a baggage
> car and two coaches, and hauled sixty people, a comfortable
> load for a packet. The fare between the above-mentioned points
> was $1.25.
>
> During the forties and fifties the immigrant travel was
> heavy, but these people were hauled specially run for that

class of passengers. They usually carried their food in the cars, and frequently the trains would stop along the road at a suitable location for them to cook and eat their meals. Some were carried in section boats, and other kind of cars, where they did their cooking and sleeping while the trains were running. It is generally supposed that Woodruff was the inventor of the sleeping cars about 1860, and that Pullman brought out the dining cars as we know them in the modern system of railroading, but the original dining and sleeping cars were used on the Old Portage twenty years and more before. The section boats had but one compartment for cooking, eating, sleeping, and storing food, a little den about 8 by 12 feet.[15]

The famous English writer Charles Dickens wrote about the Portage Railroad in his *American Notes*. He had been a passenger on the Portage RR in March of 1842. But one thing is certain, the trip up and down the mountain made an impression on him, enough to cause him to write and publish a full page or two about his experience later in 1842. In one passage he stated, "Occasionally the rails were laid upon the extreme verge of a giddy precipice; and looking from the carriage window, the traveler gazes sheer down, without a stone or scrap of fence between, into the mountain depths below. The journey is very carefully made, however; only two carriages traveling together; and, while proper precautions are taken, is not to be dreaded for its dangers."[16]

Immigrants

European immigrants made up the bulk lot of the through passenger traffic, traveling almost exclusively one way — west. This wave of traffic was an unexpected source of revenue to the Commonwealth, since the railroad was actually designed to transport freight west to east. Landing in Philadelphia, New York, or Baltimore, the immigrants would commute together on the Main Line in designated canal boats, called packets, to Hollidaysburg, and then express trains to Johnstown. From Johnstown the trip continued on the 104-mile canal portion to Pittsburgh. Because of the

Portage, immigrants could go all the way to Pittsburgh from Philadelphia—four hundred miles in four days rather than the normal three weeks or more by overland coach or wagon. In Pittsburgh, they would buy or build rafts, flat boats, or even ride on a steam-powered paddle-wheeler to their final destination.

Another important immigrant and trade route was the Cumberland Road starting in Cumberland, Maryland. Commenced in 1811, it traversed westerly through western Pennsylvania, the panhandle of Virginia, Ohio, Indiana, Illinois, to the Mississippi River. By the late 1840s it had reached all the way to Indiana. The first federally subsidized road in America, linking the east coast to the interior, it served as the first super highway in America and was sometimes referred to as "Main Street USA." But it was painfully slow and boring compared to the Ohio River. By 1850, the C&O Canal finally reached Cumberland and the National Road, making travel from Washington and Baltimore to the West a little more convenient. After 1855, the National Road faded in importance, due to the everreaching, expanding, and speedy railroads like the B&O RR, which by 1853 reached Wheeling, Virginia, and the Ohio River.

The Railroad Season

The Portage rail season spanned from early March to December 1 and was commonly known as the open period for navigation on the canal. The route could stay in operation past December 1 if the cold weather had not frozen the adjacent canals.[17] This was much better than the Erie Canal, which was usually closed by the first week of November and was at the mercy of November blizzards and copious amounts of lake-effect snow near Buffalo and Lockport from nearby Lake Erie. In the spring the Erie Canal was not open until the first week of May due to the huge amounts of snow and ice in the canal. By then the Pennsylvania Main Line had been open for over six weeks.

September in the Alleghenies brought a rush to get freight including goods such as wheat, flour, tobacco, apples, cheese, and pork across the mountain before winter. By late September, daylight lasted less than 12 hours, resulting in an abbreviated work day. By mid-October, frost could be expected on the Summit. By late November, snow started to fall, and by mid-December, the canal began to freeze. The end of the canal season and railroad season usually occurred on the same day in early to mid-December. The Portage relied on the condition of the Juniata Canal, as the *Canal Register* in Hollidaysburg reported on December 7, 1836: "The canal still continues navigable, though it was somewhat obstructed by the ice for a few days last week, in consequence of which the several lines of packets were taken off, but the freight boats continue running yet, and, judging from the present state of the weather, may probably continue to do so for some days to come."[18]

During the early years, the seasonality of the Portage was dependent on the weather and viewed as out of the operatives' control. But in later years, it was too costly to be shut down for that long a period. This seasonal shutdown would spell doom to the Portage by 1852 when another "all-weather" railroad traversed the Allegheny Mountain right parallel to that railroad.

Even when the railroad was closed for three or even four months, maintenance of the entire rail system continued. During the winter months it was time to repair the wear-and-tear of the rail season and damage caused by the natural elements. In the early years, no solid steel or iron rails existed, and pine or white oak beams with a ribbon of iron on top were used. During January and February, the extreme temperature and humidity changes caused swelling and contracting of the beams and caused the most damage. After the snow had melted during the early spring, the damage of these extreme conditions was visible, and most of the repair work could be undertaken. Due to the difference in elevation from Hollidaysburg to the Summit, a 8 to 10 degree temperature difference can be measured. It could be rainy and 40 degrees in the valley and snowing and freezing on the Summit. (Similar temperature differences were also measured by the author during several visits in the 1990s.) Thawing and rail repairs came a little later at the top than at the depots on the bottom, and sections in the shadows of the mountain or large trees could also take longer to thaw out, delaying repairs. After heavy snow melts in March large sections would appear to slide down the mountain, especially after a heavy spring rain and when the soft soil was warming up. This seemed to occur every year at different locations. Maintenance crews on the Portage repairing the line had very secure jobs for years on end.

The First Financial Numbers

Only few detailed and exact records exist of the revenues and expenses of the Allegheny Portage RR. Some historians contend that the true numbers of revenues and expenses were never compiled as accurately as the public (and tax payers) would have wanted and displayed anything but "peace and prosperity." The politicians of the day were too embarrassed to spill the beans on big fancy projects that failed. "Cooking the books" is nothing new to this century or the previous two. This has been a serious bone of contention for railroad researchers from the 1830s to the 21st century. This book is no exception. Using the numbers provided by Henry V. Poor, Esq. in a 1860 *American Railroad Journal* report (see appendix as a start) the public works project—the Allegheny Portage Railroad—appeared to not only work as planned but turned a small profit in the 1830s. From 1834 to 1839 the Portage net profits were $18,526, just what the Democrats in Harrisburg wanted! In 1836, about 30,000 cars were routed over the mountain. Despite the economic "panic" of 1837, a net profit of $13,894 appeared during the next two seasons of 1838 and 1839. In 1838, the Portage was closed most of the summer due to a huge rainstorm in June that washed out a great deal of the canal system, costing thousands of dollars and taking months to rebuild. It wasn't until November that the whole system was back in operation again and somehow showed a profit. Conversely, the cost to ship produce dropped too. In 1835, it cost $14 to transport a barrel of flour from Pittsburgh and Philadelphia. In 1800, it would have cost $120 to $220 for the same and taken over two weeks.[19] The Main Line Canal System was having a real impact on the economy.

Chapter Four
Contacts and Contracts

Rhyme of the Rail —

> Singing through the forests,
>   Rattling over ridges,
> Shooting under arches,
>   Rumbling over bridges,
> Whizzing through the mountains,
>   Buzzing o'er the vale, —
> Bless me! this is pleasant,
>   Riding on the Rail!

> — John G. Saxe, Humorist and Poet (1816–1887)

The future of Cambria County and its Portage people looked bright and pleasant for everyone — "riding on the rail" in the 1830s. Before the railroad and even before the turnpike was completed in 1820, the population was only 3,287 people. New and improved roads and the new railroad were finally bringing prosperity to the once remote mountain colony. During the 1830s, Cambria County's population grew 59 percent from 7,076 to 11,256 inhabitants in just 10 years. From 1834–1839, the Allegheny Portage Railroad showed a net profit of $18,526.[1] Even the economic panic of 1837 and the Flood of 1838 did not seem to slow down the railroads' financial success. During the spring of 1840, the Portage Railroad was ready to take off financially and politically. But that did not happen. By the end of the 1840 rail season, the Portage RR lost over $100,000 in revenue. This was an unspeakable loss for just one season. Although revenue increased 10.5 percent from 1839–1840, expenses nearly doubled. The following year,

54

1841, things appeared to be back in the black. Expenses were near normal again and a meager profit of $11,000 was shown, but new and unstable economic and political trends began to emerge in the 1840s in Pennsylvania. Could the Portage Railroad and Main Line Canal system survive as a business or would it collapse in ruin?

Horsepower

By 1839, Rowland Humphreys was a railroad contractor, of a different sort. He was hired to provide horsepower to the incline planes during the 1839–1843 rail seasons. Although steam engines, both stationary and moving, were employed along the route, horses still pulled the cars between the incline planes on some levels. It seemed like an odd mix of resources, but it worked for the most part because of the inexhaustible number of horses. Most of these contracts were along levels Nos. 6 & 7, and Nos. 7 & 8.[2]

In the spring of 1842, Rowland also had contracts for "hauling passenger cars up Incline No. 6, and hauling clay to Inclines No. 6, 7, and 8."[3] Rates charged by the contractors in 1839 were between 56 and 60 cents per day per horse, and the same per driver. Other contractor rates were as high as $1.00 per horse per day and 87$\frac{1}{2}$ cents per driver per day. Still other rates were computed per car at 6$\frac{3}{4}$ cents per car. The contract with the Motive Power Division would spell out the payment system with the selected contractor. For instance, 2,500 cars traveling eastward and 2,500 cars traveling westward per month could mean a payment of $337.50 per month to the contractor.[4] Quite a sum! In comparison, Portage engineers in 1840 were making about $2.00 per day for 30 days of work, or $60.00 per month without a day off.

Hauling of the Portage RR cars was not just limited to daytime hours; sometimes nighttime hauling was authorized by the canal commissioners to move things along. After the end of a normal workday, usually just before dusk, the cars in transit were stopped and secured in place whether they had reached their final destination or not. After sundown, everything was shut down, including the steam engines, moving the cars, and the employees went home to their families. Occasionally, a few cars had to reach their destination a little quicker than daylight allowed. This included shipments of perishable goods, livestock, US mail, and special parcels, to name a few. In early May 1839, lamps were placed on the front bumpers of cars, and a driver and a team of horses sometimes hauled them to staging areas, or even the depot, farther down the track. This night hauling, sometimes contracted to Rowland Humphreys, was permitted to shorten the time it took the cars to get to their destination at the beginning of the next working day. This extra night effort helped the Portage RR speed things up a little and avoid public criticism of the railroad being just too darn slow; as during the first year, 1834, when only a single bottle-necked tract was used by hard header haulers, and no locomotives were running at all.

After several years as a successful Portage contractor, Rowland bought a 168-acre farm east of the town of Ebensburg in 1842 for $2,000.[5] The farm contained mostly grazing land for sheep and was located between Ebensburg and Summitville. It was similar to the old farms in Wales he remembered as a boy. On the same day he bought the farm, he also bought a one-quarter-acre lot (Lot #6) and a house in Summitville next to the Portage RR for $300. Summitville was located at the Summit of the Allegheny Mountain and adjacent to the railroad. As a contractor, living next to the Portage RR had its advantages. Rowland could more easily conduct his hauling business and access the rail line with his horses since he was only a few yards away. From Summitville, he continued as a contractor for horsepower between Planes 7 & 8 from 1839 to 1850. Planes 7 & 8 were six-tenths of a mile long on the eastern slope of the mountain. Add to this the fact that between 1835–1845 freight tonnage over the mountain nearly tripled from 50,000 tons in 1835 to 145,000 tons in 1845.[6] The hauling contracts to move the increasing freight tonnage were lucrative, and were not easily given up. Rowland Humphreys, who decided back in 1834 to leave the salt business in Ebensburg, was now one of the best paid contractors on the line.

The 1840s were a turbulent decade for the Portage RR. Two-year cycles of profits followed by losses seemed to emerge

CHECK ROLL—Account of Cars hauled on the level between Inclined Plane No. 4 and 8
of the Allegheny Portage Railway during the month of August 1839.

	1	2	3	4	5	6	7	8	9	10	11	12	13	14	15	16	17	18	19	20	21	22	23	24	25	26	27	28	29	30	31	Total	Contractor. Matthias & Brown, Prs. Dolls. Cts.	Dolls. Cts.
Cars Eastward																																		94 16
Cars Westward																																		97 48
																																		$191.66

I CERTIFY that I have examined the above account, and believe the same to be correct.

J. R. Humphreys

GAMBRIA COUNTY, SS.

BEFORE me, a Justice of the Peace for said county, came R. Humphreys

who being duly sworn, saith, That the above account of the number of Cars hauled on the level between Inclined Plane
No. 4 & 8 is correct.

1839 September 2nd RECEIVED of John Snodgrass, Superintendent of Transportation,
the above amount, excepting the retained per centage; being

PAID, 172.47½
RETAINED, 19.18½
$191.66

J. R. Humphreys

APRR Check Roll, 1839

throughout the decade. How could all of this happen in such a short period of time? Everything was approved, budgeted, built, and in place for this four hundred-mile system to really take off at this time—as was intended back in 1826. Newer and stronger Norris type locomotives ran on both the Portage RR and the Columbia RR, making both more efficient for the Main Line System than in the second year when only a handful of slower models existed. The spending frenzy by the Commonwealth to purchase newer and faster locomotives and the ever-increasing maintenance cost were the foundation for the state's economic collapse. During this time, ambitious plans for additional feeder and branch canals to the Main Line existed. However, due to the poor economic climate of the 1840s many great construction plans were greatly slowed down, or abandoned altogether. Money had become tight during the early 1840s due to overzealous excitement and overspeculation in canals. In the rush to compete with its arch rivals, New York and Maryland, Pennsylvania had built up a great deal of financial debt during the construction and operation of the four hundred-mile canal system. More debt than had been estimated would be accumulated.

By 1842, the state was in serious financial trouble, on the verge of bankruptcy, and even briefly considered selling some of the public works including the Portage RR, the Columbia RR, and the whole Main Line Canal system in order to get out of debt. In nine short years the engineering triumph of its day had turned into an economic tragedy. Some people attributed it to greed; others said it was gross mismanagement. Still others blamed competing canals. The reasons were endless. By 1843, a state constitution amendment was passed by unhappy citizens to change the process of selection of the Board of Canal Commissioners. Citizens felt that the board was partially responsible for the financial mess. Up to 1843, the commissioners had been appointed by the governor. The voters decided to take the appointment power away from incumbent Governor David R. Porter and make the three-man board subject to general statewide elections. Each member would run for office every three years, alternating

years in order to avoid a complete board changeover during any
one year. It was obvious that it would not be business as usual in
Harrisburg or anywhere affected by the board's decision. But
Pennsylvania was not alone in its suffering of the hangover of
"canal fever."

Future canal projects in New York and Maryland were
scrapped as their own state project debt mounted as well. But
New York was still hanging on to its Erie Canal because of the
overall traffic it commanded. In 1844, it moved 350,000 tons of
cargo from the West while the Pennsylvania Main Line transported only 75,000 tons.[7] The Pennsylvania Main Line was being
beaten badly by the Erie Canal in 1844, and there was even talk
of widening and deepening the Erie Canal to accommodate more
traffic. A different problem existed to the south. The B&O Railroad had reached Hancock, Maryland, in June 1842 and then
Cumberland on November 5, 1842. In just 15 years the B&O had

Reliance Transportation Company poster circa the 1840s.
Railroad Museum of Pennsylvania, Pennsylvania Historical and Museum Commission (PHMC)

laid 178 miles of track from Baltimore to the National Road in Cumberland, a slow but steady pace. The B&O was slowly but surely moving west toward the Ohio River. This B&O was beginning to take off with every mile it laid and every town and city with which it connected — yet another headache for Pennsylvania.

In 1844, the 11th year of its operation, the Pennsylvania Main Line was on the verge of being shut down, sold, or both. Those involved in the operation of the Portage, like the Humphreys, could only go on and hope for the best, and things did get better — but at the slow pace of a mule.

Rowland's Sons

Rowland worked in contract for the Motive Power Division of the Portage RR during the 1830s and 40s, mainly using horsepower to move the people and freight along. The Motive Power Division of the Portage RR was the division in charge of transporting the mail, people, and freight on the railroad between the depots. Rowland was not a paid Portage RR employee at that time. His sons John, David, Thomas, William, and James would work at many of the stationary engines and locomotive engines, all over the mountain line. In 1844, they were the daring young men who risked their lives and limbs on the rails. None of them had formal education beyond primary Catholic schooling. None of them had any formal engineering or mechanical experience either, but they were ambitious. Their ability to read and write was probably even more valued. It was a huge leg up on anyone who wanted a job on the Portage, or any other high-paying job for that matter. A great deal of the common laborers on the maintenance crews could not read and write and therefore did not get higher paying jobs such as engineers and assistant engineers; even if that job was more dangerous, the applicant more courageous, or the job more physically demanding.

It could be said that the Humphreys lived in one of the remotest mountain communities in the U.S., yet worked on some of the most technologically advanced equipment in the country at that time. The Humphreys brothers worked mainly at Incline

Map of Cambria County, Pa., 1846

N

CAMBRIA COUNTY

INDIANA COUNTY

BLAIR COUNTY

Carrolltown

Loretto

Ebensburg

Gallitzin
Summitville

Hollidaysburg

Munster

Turnpike Connection

Lilly

Cassandra

Duncansville

Little Juniata River

Conemaugh River

Portage

Newry

(Gap)

Conemaugh Viaduct

Jefferson (Wilmore)

Conemaugh

Summerhill
South Fork

Johnstown

Staple Bend Tunnel

SOMERSET COUNTY

BEDFORD COUNTY

- A. Portage RR Route

- Overland Turnpike

- Important Rivers

- Not to Scale

© Chris J. Lewie, 2001

Planes Nos. 2, 4, 7, 8, and 10 in the mid-1840s. They were needed just about everywhere.

More members of one family might have worked on the Portage RR, or had more contracts, but the author has yet to find them in his research. John Humphreys was the oldest of his four brothers, and the first son to work on the Portage RR. He was born in Ebensburg in 1823 and worked on the Portage first as a driver and brakeman in the early 1840s. Drivers would either sit on top of the rail cars and direct their movement or walk along the side of the moving cars and watch for trouble. Brakemen also rode on top and applied a long foot brake to slow and eventually stop the train. In 1844, at the age of 21, John was an assistant engineer making $1.25 per day at Plane No. 7. He continued as assistant engineer at No. 7 for all of the 1845 and 1846 seasons, working with Engineer John McCaffry. In December 1846, just days after his last day working on the Portage, he enlisted in the army. According to his enlistment papers into the Mexican War he was an *"Engineer."* His friend and fellow engineer at No. 7, John McCaffry, stayed behind to work on the Portage. William Humphreys was a hitcher in summer 1844 and a general laborer, repairing the water pipes to stationary engines when necessary. In 1846, he was listed as fireman for a very brief time. He may have been the driver for his father on the horse teams on the levels. David Humphreys started as a laborer at the Rigger Loaf in June 1847 during the Mexican War years. In 1848, he became a hitcher working at No. 8, then a fireman in August. Afterward, he worked as an engineer with his brother Thomas and as a fireman at No. 8 in 1849 and in 1850 on Inclines Nos. 2, 4, 8, 10. In 1846, he lived in Summitville with his parents but did not go to the Mexican War with his other three brothers. Three brothers fighting in a war was enough for any family. Thomas Humphreys worked at different jobs and locations during his short run with the Portage Railroad in 1849–50. James Humphreys may have been a driver for his father by 1849 and made coal deliveries in the early 1850s. During the Mexican War and a shortage of rail employees, their father, Rowland, worked at Plane No. 8 as a hitcher for most of 1847. This was 13 years after hauling the first ropes out to the inclines to start the line. Rowland by now was probably one of the oldest employees on the line at the age of 52 years.[8] It appeared that by then the new profession of railroading was in the Humphreys' blood, young and old, regardless of the dangers and the politics involved in running the railroad. The Humphreys, both father and sons, worked on the Portage from 1834 to the very end in 1857, probably longer than any other family.

Chapter Five
Wheels of Peace — Wheels of War

Call to all Portage Men

By December 1846, Rowland's first son, John Humphreys, worked his way up from driver in the early 1840s to brakeman, to assistant engineer in 1844, and finally engineer on the Portage. But this would be the last time he would work on the Portage until 1849. It wasn't because of his inability as an engineer — it was something altogether different. It was called the Mexican War. Engineer John Humphreys, Assistant Engineer and Fireman Thomas Humphreys, and William Humphreys from the Portage RR joined Company B of the 2nd Volunteer Infantry. John enlisted even though he had only been married a year and a half, and his wife was expecting their first child in February 1847. Thomas and William were both single and living with their parents near Summitville.

John enlisted at the Summit, Cambria County, on December 21, 1846, for the duration of the war. After John volunteered, he was soon elected first sergeant in Company B. The regiment was formed after Christmas, and traveled overland west to Blairsville, then on to Pittsburgh. In Pittsburgh, on January 7, elections were held to determine the high-ranking officers. John was elected to captain of Company B after Capt. John Geary (assistant engineer of the Portage RR) was elected to be lieutenant colonel of his regiment.[1] John was now an officer like his father, Rowland, who had served in the local militia, "The Invincibles," during the late 1820s and early 30s. He was the second generation of Welsh Americans to be elected to such an important position. But this time someone was going to war.

In the spring of 1847, a new canal season had begun and the Portage RR began operating again. The "American Highlanders" from Cambria County and the "Washington Greys" from Blair County had taken a great many of the able-bodied men from the Portage RR and the Main Line Canal System with them to the Mexican War. A total of 87 men were raised; 46 from the Summit, 15 from Hollidaysburg, 11 from Pittsburgh, 3 from Blairsville, and 1 from Johnstown, for a total of 76 local men.[2] The drafting of those men caused a tremendous labor shortage on the railroad. To fill the labor gap Rowland Humphreys, hauling contractor and father of Capt. John Humphreys, pitched in to fill a vacant spot on the line. During the war, in 1847, Rowland worked for most of the season as a hitcher at Plane No. 8, the steepest grade on the line at 9.9 percent. His job was to hitch the rail cars to the hemp rope before their climb up the mountain. It was his first and only job as a Portage employee.

Meanwhile two thousand miles away in Mexico, Capt. John Humphreys hoped that he could muster the same courage to lead men, just as he had done on the Portage working as an engineer. In his year and a half in the army, he became an able company commander, especially during the amphibious landing in Vera Cruz, and he fought in some of the most important battles including Churubusco and Cordilleras. His brother William was not so fortunate; he was killed while fighting near his brother while storming Chapultepec Castle. The castle was an important enemy stronghold at the entrance to the capital. William

Captain John Humphreys
Story, *History of Cambria County, Pennsylvania*

Humphreys was not the only Portage man killed at that battle. A total of 24 of the original 87 men in Company B, or more than one in four, who volunteered for duty were killed in action or died of disease. This included 14 killed of 46 soldiers enlisted from the Summit alone. In early October the hot war came to an end. Months of occupation followed in Mexico City until the proper officials could sign the peace treaty to end the war. In the spring of 1848, the war with Mexico was officially over and the two re-maining Humphreys brothers, Capt. John and Pvt. Thomas, and the other 61 men under his command, were coming home after a year and half absence. But would it be the same on the Portage after the war, after the death of brother William and so many men from the Summit?

In January 1849, six months after their return from Mexico, the following letter was sent to the local newspaper in Hollidaysburg:

O. A. Trangh Esqr
Editor
Hollidaysburg, Pa.
per Capt. R. Humphreys

The Volunteer Supper
In pursuance of previous arrangements, a Supper will be given at the house of Wm S. Campbell at the Summit, on Thursday Feb 3rd at 7 O'Clock P.M. to the Members of the American Highlanders who have returned from Mexico. All those wishing well towards our brave Volunteers are respectfully invited to attend and par-take of the festivities of the Occasion. Tickets to be had at the Mansion house (Summit) or from the following Gentleman Com-posing the Committee of arrangements, several distinguished speak-ers are to address the meeting.

Price of Ticket 73 cts

John Ivory
James Born
Augustin MConnell
Jas. M Riffel
Roland Humphreys

O.A. Traugh Esqr
Dr Sir
You will please give the above an insertion in this Mountain
Standard and Much Oblige Yours Truly
Jas M Riffel

Soon after this meeting in 1849,[3] Capt. John formed the "American Junior Highlanders" as part of the Pennsylvania State Militia. The "Highlanders," as they were also called, had about 75 regular members, mostly veterans from the Mexican War, who were also workers from the Portage RR. They had regular drills, uniforms, and marched in parades, including the Fourth-of-July parade. This unit included his brother Thomas, business partner James M. Riffle, and relative George Riffle. This militia unit was similar to the unit his father was in called the "Invincibles" during the 1820s and early 30s.

The Youngest Major General in the Commonwealth

One year after returning from the war, in July 1849, John was elected major general of the militia for a four-county area including Cambria County and new Blair County (which was a part of Huntingdon County prior to 1846), Somerset County, and Bedford County to the south. This was quite an honor for this young officer, engineer, and businessman but did not come without controversy and political mud raking. Elections for positions such as county commissioner, state senate, state representative, canal commissioners, and others always involved political fights that usually ended with candidates accusing each other of some illegal or immoral practice. Hardly any election of consequence occurred without the low practice of bribery. The local press relished it, and printed every word against the candidate it also happened to despise and whose victory they sought to prevent. Other local newspapers printed "pro" articles promoting their candidate and dispelling any rumors of misconduct or bribery. This exposure gave the voters very different views of the same candidate. The following is a composite of several newspaper articles from that time discussing John Humphreys' activities:

Military Election.

The following table exhibits the result of the election for military officers for this Brigade. It is not official, but as correct as we can make it, being made up from reports we have received; but we believe a correct return will not materially change it.

It is proper to state in explanation of the singular vote polled, that Capt. John Humphreys was *not* a candidate for Brigadier General and that his name was used in connection with that office contrary to his wishes and authority or consent. In fact he positively refused to permit his name to be used, and in the Highlanders and Cambria Guards. Notwithstanding his refusal, however, to be a candidate, it appears that a few of the enemies of Col. McDonald placed him on the ticket in Johnstown for the purpose of defeating that gentleman; and the returns show that the effort has signally failed.

We believe it is also due to Maj. Potts to state that he only permitted himself to be a candidate for Lieut. Colonel under the impression that Mr. Todd had declined, and that he was consequently not running in opposition to the ticket which had been placed in nomination on last Saturday evening. How this mistake occurred we are not at present prepared to say.

	Brig. Gen.	
	J. M.	J. H.
Cambria Guards,	95	—
Highlanders,	33	7
Johnstown Companies,	1	69
Summerhill Artillerists,	—	14
	129	90

(J. M. = Joseph M'Donald)

(J. H. = John Humphreys)

It will be perceived that JOSEPH M'DONALD, ANDREW TODD, JOHN LINTON and JOHN McLAUGHLIN, being the ticket nominated on last (ballet?)[4] and,

The Late Military Election.

The last Johnstown *Transcript* contains an editorial article and two communications in relation to the late Military election in this county, in which various charges of *management*, illegal voting & c., are imputed to members connected with the volunteer company in this place, and against ourself in particular. Without any intention whatever of getting in a newspaper quarrel with our neighbors of Johnstown, we merely state for the information of the public that the majority of the statements made by the writers in the *Transcript* are incorrect, having no foundation in truth. We do not believe that the discussion has been commenced on the part of our neighbors of the Transcript with a view to any beneficial results, and we *know* that Capt. John Humphreys duly appreciates the mock sympathy that is now expressed for him by a few pretended friends as a lame apology for bringing out his name contrary to his wishes or consent. As we have before stated, it is only necessary to refer to the vote polled by the two Mexican Companies, of one of which he is Captain and in which he is highly esteemed and exceedingly popular, to prove that he was not a candidate and that he would not under any circumstances permit his name to be used as such. Had he been a candidate, the result would have been very different, and it is only to the want of honor and honesty, on the part of one of the conferees, and to the base and malicious slanders that have been put in circulation by him, that all the ill feeling that may at present exist is to be attributed. We are prepared to prove at any time, when called upon, that the statements in circulation in reference to our course in the conference or immediately afterwards, are totally false, and we are charitably disposed to believe that they have been uttered by the gentleman(?) alluded to in consequence of the fact that his midnight debauchery has rendered his memory rather defective in relation to the events of that evening.

As we acknowledge the right of the defeated party to vent their spleen, we are perfectly willing that they should

make the most of it. We have now "said our say," and shall
here after have nothing more to do with the subject.[5]
and,

Military Election.

In our last we neglected to give the result of an election
for Major general held in this place on the 2d inst., by Major
John Linton and Gen. Joseph M'Donald. Capt. John
Humphreys, of the "American Highlanders," received ten
votes, being the *entire* support of those entitled to vote in
this county. We were much pleased at this result, as no man
is better entitled or more deserving of this flattering mark of
esteem and confidence than Capt. Humphreys. What has
been the result in the other counties composing this district
we have been unable to learn. If there has been no concert of
action, however, between any of them, we are of the opinion
that Capt. Humphreys is elected.[6]
followed by,

Capt. John Humphreys

We are gratified to learn that this gentleman has been
elected Major General of this Division, composed of the counties of Somerset, Bedford, Blair and Cambria. This is a high
and well deserved compliment General, consider our bea-
ver tipped *a la militair.*[7]

After the controversial election of 1849, John would hold his
title of militia general until the outbreak of the Civil War in 1861.

The Youngest Major General.

We are glad to learn that our esteemed friend Col. Brindle
has been elected Major General of the Lycoming Division of
the Volunteers. The compliment was due to his qualifications
and merits. The "Pennsylvanian" of the 28th ult in noticing
his election remarks that he is the "*youngest Major General in
the State.*" We apprehend that Major General HUMPHREYS,
of this county, is the *youngest* Major General in this Commonwealth. He is some years the junior of Gen. Brindle, and earned
the distinction he has attained by hard service in the tented

fields of Mexico. He has proven himself a daring soldier, and will make an accomplished commander.[8]

After the election, General Humphreys finally organized the "Junior American Highlanders" in October 1849. This local volunteer unit stayed together until the outbreak of the Civil War. John Humphreys would hold the militia rank of major general until that same time. But the cost of supporting an active regiment was too much and it was disbanded in 1862. Many of the meetings, dinners, and activities centered around the militia groups in the 1840s and 1850s, were held in Summitville at the Summit Mansion Hotel.

Chapter Six
Riffle & Humphreys Merchants

Know Thy Trade

After returning to their mountain home following the war in Mexico, Capt. John Humphreys and Pvt. Thomas Humphreys settled back into life surrounding the Portage RR as best they could. John, the eldest son, did not work on the Portage during the second half of the 1848 season. Neither did many of the 63 men who returned from the war expecting to continue their old jobs. During his absence John's first child, John William Humphreys, was born in April 1847. In the fall of 1848, John and his brother-in-law James M. Riffle formed a business partnership called "Riffle and Humphreys Merchants/Proprietors." At that time, James Riffle was a local merchant in Summitville. James came from a well-known local merchant family and was a Democrat like his father. John was a war hero but was without work. He did have his father's eye for business. The two joined together using John's newfound fame and James' business sense to build a respectable business. They would both rely on the Portage to transport their goods to and from their local customers.

By late 1848, "Riffle & Humphreys Merchants" were in business near the Summit Mansion Hotel along Railroad Street in Summit. One of their customers was the Portage Railroad, but they only sold them about $50.00 worth of goods in all of 1849.[1] To become prosperous was going to take some time and a different approach to selling. Since the beginning of the railroad, some merchants in Summit had been buying goods in other towns across Pennsylvania, and shipping them up to the Summit to sell them to local customers. They did so by signing releases from freight lines against "the dangers of the Rail Roads, and Canal navigation, Fire in Boats, Cars, and transhipping Depots, and incidental delays excepted."[2] Others had the same idea years earlier when coal was discovered under the mountains in mass quantities, and coal miners needed shovels, picks, and black powder to extricate it. Women wanted the latest fashions from Philadelphia, hats of all colors, housewares, silverware, and queenswear, glazed earthenware similar to China.

By spring 1849, John still needed money to support his family in Summit. So, on June 1, 1849, John joined the Portage not as an engineer but as a "state agent." State agents, also called "car agents," directed passengers and freight, and collected tolls from people using the rail route. John Humphreys received $1.50 per day.[3] This job would assure a steady income regardless of the sluggish merchant business. On June 27, 1849, approximately one year after John's return, this letter was received at Summitville:

Villa Nova College June 27th, /49

Dear Friend James,

I have at length got a letter commenced for you. I intended to write every week for the last two months , but as you are already aware I never accomplished it. The only excuse I can offer is that I was uncertain whether you were at home or on your way to the city; as the last letter I received from the Summit, stated you were about to start shortly for Goods. However I will throw myself on your indulgence hoping you will excuse my negligence.

I assure you I am very grateful to you for the papers you sent. They were so acceptable, that I read them over at least a dozen of times. From the names attached to the papers, I presume that you and Capt. Humphreys have entered into partnership. If such be the case, allow me to present you with my best wishes for your future success. Of which, I have not the least doubt from the popularity of you both, and from your individual fitness for business.

This is quite a change of life for me, and was rather unpleasant at first, but I have become accustomed to it, and am well satisfied with it. However I will delay a description of it until I have the pleasure of seeing you which I hope to have in about four weeks.

This day three weeks is our distribution day which will last for about six weeks. I need not a four [?] you that I am very anxious to return to the mountain, and see you all once more. The weather here is extremely warm, much more so than over I felt it on the mountain, in fact it has been so hot, that last week two men in this neighborhood died from the effect of the heat.

Well James I must bring this uninteresting letter to a close, in consequence of not having any more news to communicate to you. Please give my respects to all my friends, especially to R. Doncaster Wm Ivory, Brock Boon Henry Maloy, Chas Fances, Da McColgan + Peter Dougherty + to all the fairer sex

Please ask Wm Iy + Brock B. to answer my last + Allow me to subscribe myself over Your Friend

J. C. Noon

P. S.

Please write soon write anything and everything J. C. N.[4]

Then, two days later from another Noon.

Saturday (June 29, 1849)

Mr. James Riffle

My Dear Friend

I received the Captains very kind this evening and Reply to it immediately, tell our kind Captain I would like to go very much and celebrate the glorious fourth with my old companions but it would be impossible for me to go now as I would have to have expense money, and Father is not prepared at present to give it to me   he is very anxious for me to go and that is all that prevents me give my love to Alice and all my old acquaintance and tell them not to forget me   please answer immediately   ever your friend

Albert Noon

even if I was prepared to go I would be afraid to by myself

PS Amanda has come home   her and Marie send their complements to you

Direct your next letter to Mount Union[5]

The first business year of Riffle & Humphreys Merchants, 1849, was one of the best for the Portage as well. The war years were the Portage's biggest years in both tonnage and profits. In

1849, 34,611 loaded cars and 12,381 empty cars were cleared and were sent westward over the Portage road. Also, 817 section boats were carried over the Portage road westward, and 802 eastward. The whole through-tonnage carried over the road during the year amounted to 143,294 tons.[6]

The busy Portage also purchased items from the two new merchants. They bought shovels, hand files of all sorts, corn brooms, screws and hinges, white lead, red lead, writers ink, linseed and sperm oil, borax, sealing wax, paste board, augers, chalk, axe handles, buckets, two-foot rulers, glass, sandpaper, kegs of black powder, and candles.

Their Second Year, 1850

Riffle & Humphreys' second year as merchants was more successful than their first. Between 1830 and 1850, Cambria County's population more than doubled, from 7,076 in 1830 to 17,773 in 1850.[7] In January 1850, James M. Riffel bought Lot No. 30 in Summitville from Thomas Jackson (and others), along south side of Railroad Street.[8] This crossroad of the railroad and the turnpike was an excellent location. Then, Riffle & Humphreys advertised their new business in the local newspaper. And finally, they received larger Portage RR contracts than in 1849. The merchants also brought in finished goods from Philadelphia and Pittsburgh, first by canal then finally rail that was unique to this rural and mountainous area. Riffle & Humphreys were one of the few merchants in the Alleghenies to use both canal and railroad for their retail business. Most merchants were accustomed to waiting for goods to arrive by way of the turnpike. By then the 30-year-old overland turnpike was being used primarily for the transportation of slower, bulky materials such as coal, lumber, stone, or barrels of salt. It was still an important link to Ebensburg or Hollidaysburg as a farm-to-market route and in the winter time one of the only routes through the mountains for horsedrawn sleds.

Riffle and Humphreys helped to bring Philadelphia to the Alleghenies. They were some of the first businessmen in the region to use the railroad to bring in finished goods for sale. Riffle

Local newspaper advertisement, 1840s

DRY GOODS!

Just received, a general assortment of seasonable goods, consisting of Cloths, Cassimeres, Sattinetts, *Muslins,* Tickings, Flannels, Ginghams, Cashmeres, and a large stock of

PRINTS

cheaper than any heretofore offered to the public, together with a great variety of

Shawls,
Gloves,
Hosiery, Woollen Yarns,
& Carpet chains.

BOOTS & SHOES: A general assortment, such as Men's coarse and fine Boots, Ladies Slippers, walking shoes, Gums, and Children's Shoes.

CAPS: Men's cloth, Boy's cloth, and Oil cloth, and Children's velvet.

Queensware,
Hardware,
Groceries,
Lumber, & Shingles.

For sale by   J. M. HEWIT.

Hollidaysburg, Oct. 21, 1346.

Local newspaper advertisement, 1840s

& Humphreys stuck to the basics like dry goods, food, clothing, and hardware, although other merchants brought in exotic food items such as fresh oysters and fish from the Chesapeake Bay. Soon the two men were filling orders for clothing, silverware, and queensware, and traveling back and forth to and from Philadelphia and Pittsburgh to keep up with the demand. "Why go to Philadelphia, the cultural center of America, if it can come to you?" was the catch phrase.

In 1849, Riffle & Humphreys sold about $50.00 worth of goods to the Portage RR. In 1850, they sold about $500.00 worth of goods, about 10 times more than in 1849.[9] This did not include the $50.00 rent for an office for the supervisor of the Motive Power Division for most of 1850. They also were contractors for fuel or "Cord Wood" in 1850, "For 100 Cords Wood delivered Between Planes No. 3 + 4 in July at $1.25 - $125.00," and "For 100 Cords Wood delivered on Level Between Planes 3 + 4 in Sept - @ $1.25 $125.00."[10]

Pennsylvania Railroad Contracts

In 1851, the Pennsylvania Railroad Company was constructing a rail line from the Juniata Valley up the Allegheny Mountain and over to Pittsburgh. In doing so they also needed common supplies to complete their job. They purchased supplies from Riffle & Humphreys when they were near Summit building the line through nearby Cresson Springs. Everyday items such as candles, brooms, soap, hats, mapping paper, and food stuff like cheese, raisins, and coffee, were needed by the workmen constructing the Western Division and Mountain Division of the

Pennsylvania Railroad. See appendix. But those small contracts were not enough to survive against all the other newcomers and established businessmen in town.

Dissolution

The Riffle & Humphreys enterprise lasted until the end of 1851.[11] Only James Riffle renewed the contract for office space with the Portage supervisor in August. It is uncertain why the partnership did not last very long. The reasons for the Riffle & Humphreys breakup are as endless as the ropes on the incline. James was in the process of completing his purchase/indenture on the Summit Hotel. John wanted to be back on the Portage as an engineer.

After the business breakup in early 1852, the Engineering Office of the New Portage rented an office from James Riffle for "Avoidance of Inclined Planes, on the APRR." James Riffle then purchased the Summit Hotel and continued to work as a contractor for the Portage. After buying out his partner, John Humphreys continued as both an engineer and a clerk in his own store along Railroad Street in Summitville.

James Riffle continued to rent his offices to the Portage supervisors and may have even served as a clerk on the Portage in 1852. Prior to the construction of the New Portage RR the Engineering Office and the supervision of the Motive Power Division both rented offices from James M. Riffle in 1851 and 1852.[12]

Chapter Seven
The Summit Mansion Hotel

"In fact, the place most frequently referred to in contemporary documents is the 'Summitt House,' 'Riffles,' or perhaps 'Denlinger's.'" The opening of the railroad was celebrated there and the 42-room hotel was the meeting place for general festivities.[1] The Summit Mansion Hotel was built between 1832–1833 by either Thomas Jackson or William Kinnear at the crossroads of the Huntingdon, Cambria & Indiana Turnpike and the newly constructed Portage RR. By December 1833, the hotel was open for business as a crossroads inn for both the existing turnpike traffic and the soon-to-be Portage RR traffic.

The hotel was built at an elevation of 2,314 feet above sea level, and just a few yards from the actual Summit of Allegheny Mountain, leading to the name "Summit Mansion Hotel." Built next to the existing turnpike, the hostelry served overland stage travelers going either east to Hollidaysburg or west to Ebensburg and beyond. Being located near the new railroad would create even more business for the hostelry, especially if passenger cars stopped in front before moving to the next plane or level.

The Summit Hotel was a large and grand hotel for its time. The three-story wood frame hotel had smooth pine siding and was probably painted white during the Portage RR years. It was "three stories tall, had eight-foot ceilings, long hallways, contained 42 rooms each furnished with a bed, dresser and washstand to hold a basin and pitcher."[2] Some of the rooms contained fireplaces which got much use on cold mountain nights. The first floor consisted of the lobby, front desk, parlor, dining/meeting room, and kitchen in the rear. The kitchen had an early form of indoor water that was piped in from a local iron spring. Captain Humphreys and the "American Junior Highlanders" often met in the dining room for their local militia meetings during the 1840s and 1850s.[3] Most of the sleeping rooms were on the second floor with larger state rooms in the corners facing the turnpike; additional sleeping rooms were on the third floor. Also on the third floor was a billiards room that doubled as an extra general meeting room. A tavern, wine cellar, and store were on the ground floor. Because running water was only piped into the kitchen, outhouses were located to the rear of the lot near the horse stable and wash house.

Unlike the Portage RR, which was closed from December to March, the hotel was open year round for business. During the winter months, when the Portage was closed because of frozen canals, only overland stages and travelers on horseback and in horse-drawn sleds would frequent the hotel. After the spring snow melted and the railroad reopened, the first passenger cars would pass by. During the operating season, passenger trains would stop near the doorstep of the hotel for easy pickup and delivery. This "hitching post" service provided an added boost to the hotel's business. For those passengers who did not visit the hotel or tavern, the trains would stop to allow them to buy readymade food items prepared in the hotel kitchen.

Hotel Ownership

The hotel did well under different owners and landlords throughout the Portage years. Eleven years after the hotel began operating, Thomas Jackson sold it to Phillip Noon in 1844. Mr. Noon then quickly sold it to William J. Campbell about 1845. Mr. Campbell sold it to James M. Riffle in December 1853 in an indenture, near the end of the Portage days.[4] The Riffles were probably the fourth owners, and by far retained possession of the hotel for the longest period of time during the mid-1800s. During their ownership the Riffle and the Humphreys family used the hotel as a central meeting place. Discussions of business, politics, religion, and the railroad could always be heard in the dining and meeting rooms. Following the Civil War, it became the family's Christmastime gathering place.

The Summit Mansion Hotel, built about 1832, was one of the most famous hotels in the region. It was located conveniently at the intersection of the turnpike and Portage Railroad, at the summit of Allegheny Mountain. Trains stopped here to load and unload passengers, and the hotel was a place of community and civic gatherings. The Riffles, in-laws of the Humphreys, owned it from 1853 to 1872. John Humphreys' son, John W., was raised here during the early 1860s.

APRR National Historic Site

Summitville

The village of Summitville was always viewed as the top of Allegheny Mountain. The Summit Mansion House was located in the very center of the village and along Level No. 6. Summitville had grown from zero inhabitants in 1830 to over two hundred people in 1840, which can be attributed to the railroad. It was not uncommon for local social, political, railroad, and militia gatherings to be held in various hotels or taverns throughout the village. By 1850 the village had doubled in population to 406 people.[5] According to records Washington Township had eight hotels, four in Summitville and another four outside of town. Five boarding houses were located outside of

Summitville. Another famous hotel not listed in Washington Township, the Lemon House, was located east along the turnpike in Blair County. The inhabitants of Summitville in 1850 were mostly Portage rail workers, coal miners, laborers, lumbermen, farmers, and sheepherders. Some Portage employees such as state agents, engineers, riggers, and laborers are listed as living or boarding at the Summit House. The office of the Motive Power Division of the Railroad was located in the village for easy access downhill to the railroad in either direction.

In November 1850, the first description of the hotel and its location appeared:

For Sale or Rent.

The subscriber offers for sale to the 31st of December next, and if not sold by that time will rent on advantageous terms the "SUMMIT MANSION HOTEL."

This fine Hotel is located ten miles from Hollidaysburg and nine miles from Ebensburg at a point where the Turnpike Road leading from Hollidaysburg to Pittsburg crosses the Allegheny Portage Rail Road, and consequently receives the patronage of the traveling public that crosses either of these thoroughfares to Philadelphia or Pittsburg. Four trains of passenger cars stop at the door daily in the business season, and from five to ten coaches in the winter.

The pure atmosphere, pure water, and delightful scenery of the Allegheny Mountains, make this a most desirable summer resort for citizens of Philadelphia and Pittsburg, and as many permanent visitors can be had as the House will accommodate.

The building is spacious and admirably arranged for a Hotel and has been recently refitted, painted and enlarged. An excellent Stable, carriage house, wash house and convenient out-door buildings are on the premises and also a neat tenant house for servants.

If the premises are sold, a clear and indisputable title will be made, and possession given on the first day of April next.

The undersigned begs leave through this advertisement to return his hearty acknowledgments to his numerous friends for the many favors bestowed on him and assures them that nothing but sickness in his family has induced him to relinquish a claim to their patronage.

Wm. S. CAMPBELL

Summit, Nov. 25, 1850-9[6]

Most of the buildings in Summitville, including the Summit Hotel, were built of wood from local oak and hemlock trees. The hotel was almost lost to fire in June 1852, but was saved by alert citizens.[7]

Guest of Note

Numerous notables stayed at the hotel during the Portage years and beyond. Future general and president, Ulysses S. Grant, lodged there in mid-May 1839 on his way to West Point as a cadet. President-elect William H. Harrison boarded there in December 1839 en route to the Whig National Conference in Harrisburg and January–February 1841 on his way to Washington for his inauguration. The Portage was probably closed for the season. Several months after his death his body was transported back to Cincinnati, Ohio, from Washington, utilizing the Portage route through the mountains and passing the Summit Hotel for a second time. The famous English writer Charles Dickens stayed there in March 1842 on his tour of America and commented on the operation of the Portage (see *American Notes* in earlier chapter). Another guest was Congressman and Whig Abraham Lincoln (Illinois), sometime between 1847–1849; he later became the 16th president of the United States.[8] Jenny Lind, Swedish opera singer, roomed at the hotel sometime between 1850–1852. While under the management of promoter P. T. Barnum she toured the United States for two years. In America she was paid $1,000 a night to perform, for 150 nights.[9] It is not certain whether she was paid $1,000 when she broke into song on top of the Summit before her stay. Another former president to travel past the hotel was President Zachary Taylor. "When President Taylor died in Washington on July 9, 1850, his body was brought over the mountains on the Portage Railroad,

Summit Mansion Hotel as it looked in the 1950s. Jack Seabolt, *left*, and Roy Mangold, *right*. Sadly, the Summit Hotel was destroyed in a fire in 1980.

Photo courtesy of Brenda Franco

and taken from here on the Canal, 'Old Whitey,' the general's favorite saddle horse that had been with him in his campaign in Mexico, leading the cortege as it came down Railroad street."[10] Taylor was the second president to die in office. The first was William H. Harrison, a Whig, who also stayed in the Summit Hotel. A foreign dignitary to stay there was Lajos Kossuth, the Hungarian patriot, on January 17, 1852. The ex-Hungarian leader was in America raising money for Hungarian independence.

In 1852, William S. Campbell, owner of the hotel, was also the supervisor of the Motive Power Division of the Portage RR. On December 16, 1853, James M. Riffle bought the Summit Hotel from him for $2,700. James and his wife would own it and Lot #1 for the next 20 years until his death in 1872. It also included in the Deed "...And to have also exclusive right to the use of the water of the Spring near the turnpike east of the Summit Hotel herefore taken by pipes to the Said Hotel."[11] It is unclear why Mr. Campbell sold the 20-year-old hotel other than for health reasons.

The hotel was facing some real problems in its future. The first was the fear that its business would suffer greatly with the completion of the new Pennsylvania RR line in Cresson a mile away. And second, the proposed construction of the New Portage railroad that would bypass the Summitville area entirely as it rounded the Summit instead of crossing it. Cresson Springs was going to be the new location of the Portage line with two new rail stations: one for the Pennsylvania RR next to the turnpike, and one for the New Portage railroad nearby. The two new stations a mile away and all downhill in Cresson Springs meant that Summit Hotel might be overlooked as the weary travelers would not be eager to walk uphill a mile on a 10-percent grade after their long rail voyages. James Riffle bought the hotel anyway and saw to it that he provided a carriage ride to the top when passengers arrived at the station, bypassing other closer hotels along the way. In 1855 another Portage hotel, "The Mountain House," located in Hollidaysburg, was dismembered, brought up the mountain in pieces, and rebuilt in Cresson for the use of the Pennsylvania RR higher-ups. Instead of dwindling, the hotel business in the area seemed to be booming. The Summit Hotel appeared to have been built in the right place at the right time.

Chapter Eight
Accidents and Snake Heads

Accidents and injuries occurred on the Portage RR more often than one might think. Although no accurate records were ever maintained by the Board of Canal Commissioners, newspapers, for 25 years, reported some horrible accidents. Between the years 1841–1854, 34 people were involved in accidents that resulted in death.[1] In 1850, 8 people were listed as killed in separate accidents.[2] The same number were killed in 1851. Some of these accidents and deaths were caused by inattentive people unaccustomed to the operation of a railroad, others were caused by the slipping or even snapping of the hemp ropes, and still others by a loose slab of iron from the rails prying the bottom off a passenger car in transit. While some accidents were not serious and not reported in the local newspaper, others more severe or involving important persons, were worthy of newsprint. Just as during elections, the more intriguing a story was the more ink it got in Ebensburg, Hollidaysburg, or Johnstown.

The writers for the local newspapers did their very best to describe the gruesome details of a railroad accident to readers. Colorful depictions used by the writers included: "melancholy accident," "a most lamentable accident," "a most terrible accident," "a most shocking accident," "there was a regular smash up," "mortally injuring no less than three persons," "killed in minutes," "died 20 minutes after," and "instantly hurried into eternity."[3] Daring newspaper reporters described injured passengers and workers as "pared to the bone," "mangling them in a most shocking manner, and injuring him overwise," "crushed to death in an awful manner," "smashing two or three of them to atoms," "crushing it so shockingly as to render amputation necessary," "amputation necessary to save life," "the flesh on one of his thighs is horribly lacerated," and "shockingly crushed both legs," to name a few.

Editors described the condition of accident survivors as "the sufferer is doing well," "he lingered for about ten hours," or "to leave no hopes of his recovery." Several local doctors, including Dr. James Christy, performed amputations of mangled limbs to save accident victims' lives. If the "melancholy accident" victim survived the accident, the surgery, and any post-operative infection, then that fortunate person resumed a somewhat normal life without a hand or a foot. If the surgery and amputation was unsuccessful the families would "mourn his untimely end."[4] Following are some articles depicting such railroad accidents:

> Oct 6, 1841: **Melancholy Accident.** On Saturday last, as William Moore, who had been until recently a clerk at Huntingdon Furnace, in this county, and originally of the city of Philadelphia, in attempting to jump on the end of one of the Four Section Car Boats, near the Summit Tavern, on the Allegheny Portage railway, fell, and two of the wheels of the heavy truck passed over his right arm and leg, mangling them in a most shocking manner, and injuring him otherwise. *Dr. Christy* of his place, was in attendance, but in consequence of the extensive injury, medical of surgical aid was of no avail. He retained his senses until the last, and calmly expired about two hours after receiving the accident.[5]

> Sept. 1, 1847: **Accidents on the Rail Road.** We have this week the painful duty of recording a couple of sad accidents on the Portage Road. On Saturday last, a man named *Wm. Morgan*, was killed instantly on the road near the Weigh-Scales in Gaysport, by being caught between two trucks and crushed. Mr. M. resided at the head of Plane 10, and has left a wife and several children to mourn his untimely end. On yesterday morning, owing to the breaks on the truck being out of order, a Section Boat named 'Sam'l P. Funk,' of Harrisburg, ran down the grade between No. 10 and Hollidaysburg,

and opposite the U.S. Hotel came in contact with a train of Cars belonging the Penna. & Ohio Line, smashing two or three of them to atoms and wrecking considerably three more. There were several persons on the boat, but all escaped injury save one, a passenger named Andrew Cassiday, an Irishman, from the city of Baltimore. He was sitting on the front part of the truck, and had the fingers and thumb of one hand torn off, and was otherwise considered injured.[6]

Sept. 26, 1850: **Accident.** Mr. Edward Daley a hitcher at Plane #2 was killed 9/18. Sitting on hind end of car descending plane—fastenings or stops gave way—car traveled to foot with tremendous rapidity and struck another car—Knocked him off—Killed—left family with five small children. Source: *Mountain-Sentinel,* Thursday, Sept. 26, 1850.[7]

"Snake Heads"

One type of accident was unique to passengers riding inside a rail car. Sometimes the long, thin iron strip on top of the stringers (wooden rails) would come loose and poke through the floor of a passenger car in transit. These iron strips, or "snake heads" as they were called, could prove to be both terrifying and amazing as they would slice through the wooden car floor in any direction, causing the passengers to dance a jig while trying to avoid the jagged metal ribbon that looked like the head of a striking snake. Passengers' legs were in danger of being severely cut if they did not respond quickly enough to the subterranean danger. In later years, the Portage employed all iron rails, avoiding the infamous snake heads danger altogether. Passengers were overjoyed with this innovation, to say the least.

Other dangers included getting caught in the stationary engines' machinery, or exploding boilers, as happened on April 28, 1847:

EXPLOSION OF A LOCOMOTIVE BOILER. On Thursday last, between Planes 1 and 2, on the Allegheny Portage railroad, near the tunnel, the boiler of the Locomotive "Bush Hill" bursted, and killed instantly, the engineer, JAMES PATTERSON, and very seriously injured JAMES BARON,

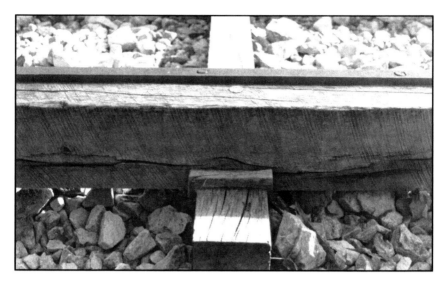

Wooden rails or "stringers" were first used on the railroad with iron straps affixed on top. The wood for the rails was easy to cut and shape and was found in abundance in the mountains. Harder woods such as oak and ash were preferred over pine, as they were stronger and more durable.

Iron rails were used later on the Portage Railroad. They could support more weight, were more durable than the old wooden rails, and ended the danger of "snake heads," iron straps that loosened and penetrated the rail car floors. Passengers were pleased with this solid iron innovation. Here the iron rail is secured to stone sleepers.

formerly of Pittsburg, who was on the engine with Mr. Patterson; and less seriously JOHN DAVIS, fireman. Mr. P. was on his way to his bother-in-law's funeral, and Mr. Baron was to supply his place for a day on the Locomotive. Mr. Baron's skull was badly fractured, and his recovery a matter of much doubt. Mr. Patterson left a wife and family near the scene of the disaster, to mourn his untimely end. How true it is that "in the midst of life we are in death." and that we know not what hour may bring forth![8]

In 1852 an accident to Engine #6 was reported:

BOILER BURSTED. — On Tuesday of last week, one of the boilers at the head of plane No. 6 Allegheny Portage Railroad, exploded, doing great damage to the building and mortally injuring no less than three persons, and severely hurting one or two more. The names of the deceased persons are, Owen Reily and Matthew Pursell, firemen, and Felix Handlin, a laborer. The boiler had been in use about 15 years, and was worn out long ago. The other engine being in order the cars passed the plane as usual on the same evening.[9]

This explosion at Plane No. 6 occurred prior to the invention of boiler gauges. Engine #6 was later rebuilt and re-placed on line for service. It is uncertain whether steam gauges were ever installed on any of the stationary engines. Those were the everyday working dangers.

Lightning and Fire!

Then there was lightning! The risk of being hit by lightning on top of one the highest peaks in the region was much higher than in the adjacent Juniata Valley. Add to that equation the high amounts of steel and iron used in the locomotives and stationary engines, and 36 miles of rails, and you have a lightning rod of biblical proportions. Lightning could kill instantly, even if you were a few feet away from the contact or "bolt"; and it was impartial.

Fire, an everyday danger, was just as impartial as lightning. It could destroy a lifetime of hard work and profits in minutes, and often did. The Summit Hotel almost burned to the ground in

June 1852 because of an adjacent barn fire. Flash floods were another danger. Floods were common in the spring and early summer months in the mountains; a large flood in June 1838 closed the whole Main Line down for several months after the rains had washed away canal work near Hollidaysburg. (The largest flood in the area occurred on May 31, 1889, known as the infamous "Johnstown Flood," when an old Portage dam, converted for private recreation, broke above Johnstown.)

Dozens of accidents, dismemberments, and deaths on the Portage RR went unreported in the local newspapers. Newspapers usually wrote about the severe accidents instead of the minor incidences, such as losing a finger or toe. Other deaths may not have made the newspapers because the victims were unknown travelers or vagrants. Working on the Portage or any other railroad in the early years was a dangerous occupation regardless of the pay or prestige of being a hitcher or an engineer. Accidents happened weekly or monthly. Diseases were quite different. They could be an everyday health problem for anyone in the area of a general epidemic including railroad employees, local citizens, and passengers. Epidemics included tuberculosis, influenza, dysentery, smallpox, consumption, and cholera.

Cholera

Asiatic cholera seemed to break out every summer near the Portage and its canals, as early as the 1830s, and was especially strong in the summers of 1847, 1848, and 1849. Although not truly associated with the railroad, cholera was often found in the canal basins next to the railroad. This illness usually started in the Southern states in the early spring and worked its way north with the warmer weather. Cholera is a waterborne disease, and the extensive canal systems in America at that time promoted its spread. Not knowing the cause of the quickly spreading disease, people could not prevent nor treat that sickness. Quack treatments like warm salt baths did little to cure a patient and often caused dehydration and death.

In the summer of 1848, when John Humphreys and his brother Thomas returned from the Mexican War, a cholera epidemic broke out near Johnstown just a few miles west of their home, creating delays on the Main Line for fear of spreading the deadly disease. In early July 1850, cholera took the life of President Zachary Taylor just days after he attended a ceremony of the new Washington Memorial on July 4, 1850. Cholera was so widespread it stretched as far west as the upper regions of the Missouri River and the Rocky Mountains—one thousand miles away. For that reason, it was hard to predict when and where it would strike next. It is understandable that people were afraid of it every summer:

> **Cholera**—The following statement, if true may be valuable in the treatment of cholera, and no doubt is the origin of the paragraph that has been making the rounds of the papers. Two men employed in extracting salt from the lake in the neighborhood of Saltzburgh, were attacked by the disease, and left by their medical attendant as incurable. Their bodies had become completely black, when the overseer of the work undertook to cure them. He heated a quantity of water from one of the salt lakes to a very high degree, and placed one of the dying men in the bath. After being in half an hour, the man recovered his senses and expressed how delightful were his sensations. Upon this the other sufferer was put into a similar bath. By degrees their bodies turned from black to purple, then red, and at the end of three hours they assumed their natural colour, and the men were free from the disease. It may be beheved, that the pores, being opened by the heat, absorbed the saline particles, which mingled with the blood and liquified it. This corresponds with the known effects of salt upon coagulated blood.[10]

> **Cholera**. The ravages of this dreadful scourge are still on the increase. It is making its appearance on both sides of us as near as Huntingdon and Pittsburg, and we learn from Hollidaysburg *Register* that a death from Cholera occurred at Plane No 10, A.P.R.R. on Monday last. We are disposed to believe that some other disease was the cause of his death. The subject, however, is said to have been an intemperate man who had been indulging in his cups freely for several

days. He was seized at 8 or 9 o'clock in the morning, and died about 3 o'clock of the same day. We also learned that three fatal cases of Cholera occurred in Alexandria, Huntingdon county on Sunday last. The subjects were a contractor on the Central Railroad, and two of his workmen.[11]

Other newspaper articles described cholera differently:

With the canal came ague, euphoniously called "Juniata Jigs" by some of the newspapers. There were many cases during the warm weather, and when it got a strong grip on a man "he shook till his teeth rattled." The apothecaries were kept busy dispensing quinine and ague bitters to cure the dreaded disease.[12]

Cholera was not unknown to the Humphreys. For the most part they had avoided contracting it by drinking well water. But one brother was not so lucky and in 1852 was killed by that disease while out of state. Summit Hotel Register Book: *Monday Morning June 28, 1852, Thomas Humphreys Died of Cholera on 7th or 8th June – Dubuque Iowa.*[13] Thomas, survivor of the Mexican War as was his brother John, did not survive the cholera war back home. He became another casualty of disease in America. He was the second Humphreys son to die in five years.

Other threats to the people along the Portage and the canals included poisonous snakes, rabid animals, mountain lions, hungry raccoons and black bears, ticks, lice, biting flies, gnats, intestinal parasites, and a host of other unenjoyable mountain critters like skunks, ground hogs, and opossums. The everyday critters weren't as scary as Asiatic cholera, but an unpleasantry to everyone nonetheless. The new railroad technology, although great and mighty, could do nothing to solve these everyday problems.

Chapter Nine
The Pennsylvania Railroad Company

The Old Portage RR

The year 1850 was the beginning of the end for what was to be called the "Old Portage Railroad." After 15 years of extensive use of the 10 inclines/planes, and levels, the railroad was in deplorable shape. The years of moving tons of material and tens of thousands of people every year had taken its toll. Boilers were exploding, accidents were way up, and people were getting killed while using the railroad. Between 1850 and 1851, 16 people were killed in railroad accidents. Something had to be done. Repairs to an entire 36-mile incline system, that was already outdated, seemed inconceivable. Asking for additional tax dollars for repairs on the Portage was out of the question. Letting the whole Main Line System sit idle or abandoned would mean defeat of the Keystone State and victory for New York and Maryland commerce.

By spring 1850, the Portage Railroad was just breaking even financially after 15 years' operation.[1] During the entire 1840s a very meager profit of $9,268 was produced after all the state financial turmoil involving state projects and incurred debts (see appendix). The Portage never showed a profit for more than two years in a row, and it never showed a loss for three years in a row. The years 1846–1849, which included the Mexican War, immigrant traffic, and gold rush traffic, netted the canal commissioners a sum of $154,048 — its best net return of any four-year period. The system actually made money for the Canal Commission during this brief period (Poor, ARJ 1860 Report). By 1849 the Portage was just breaking even, and citizens of the Commonwealth, including Governor William F. Johnson, the only Whig governor during the operation of the Main Line System, started to think much differently about the whole state-owned and -operated system. It was always up and down on the Allegheny Mountain—in more ways than one.

To compound the problem, the C&O Canal in Maryland had just reached Cumberland—a distance of 197 miles from Georgetown, Virginia—and was only 120 miles from its goal, the Ohio River. So far it had cost $11,000,000, with the last leg—from Hancock to Cumberland, a distance of 62 miles—taking a whopping 11 years to construct and millions of dollars to build.[2] This included a 3,118-foot-long canal tunnel, called Paw Paw Tunnel, through Tunnel Hill, Maryland, that had finally been completed and was open for canal traffic. In Cumberland, the C&O Canal could either link up to the Cumberland Road, which ventured beyond Illinois, or it could link up with the B&O Railroad. Cumberland was quickly becoming the new Pittsburgh or gateway to the West, although not quite on the beloved Ohio River as Pittsburgh was.

The B&O RR had reached Cumberland in 1843 and was still laying tracks west. By 1850, it had shipped 230,338 tons of freight to Baltimore. A majority of that was 132,534 tons of coal and 54,636 tons of flour.[3] Ten years prior it had only shipped 60,503 tons or one-quarter of the load in 1850 from lines built short of Cumberland; 42,383 tons of that were flour and no coal.[4] What would happen when it reached the Ohio River?

To the north was still more trouble. The Buffalo & Albany Railway had been built from Albany to Buffalo, New York, a distance of 327 miles. It paralleled the entire Erie Canal along the Mohawk Valley and became the Erie's new competitor for freight. Also within New York was the New York & Erie Railway along the border with Pennsylvania. It also traversed across the Empire State from the Delaware River to the coastal plain of Lake Erie. Both railways had connecting lines to New York City at their eastern terminuses, and their western terminuses along Lake Erie's shoreline to Ohio and the Midwest.

The unsettling news about the other new railways and the C&O Canal made the discussion about the future of the Portage RR that more difficult for the elected officials in charge of the state works. In 1850, the great burden, both political and financial, was about to explode like an overloaded locomotive boiler. But the state just could not walk away from this multimillion dollar project and admit defeat—not just yet! Victory was what it wanted. But how could victory be achieved?

Finally, in 1850, a new plan was placed on the drawing board in Harrisburg that had to be workable regardless of the cost. The new plan would include both a brandnew two-lane railroad, minus the inclines, and a general upgrade for the remaining original system. The daring project would be called the "New" Portage Railroad. The "New Portage" project just had to work—as the old Portage just had to work in 1832. State pride was at stake and too much was riding on it to fail. And, political heads would roll, if it failed! And so on, and so on. The proposed "New" Portage, with its expensive upgrades and overall cost, was a major problem for the Board of Canal Commissioners; another problem was, for the first time, rail competition from within the state.

By 1850, another railroad, called the "Pennsylvania Railroad," was creeping up the Juniata Valley from Harrisburg toward the Summit. Chartered in 1846 by Philadelphia businessmen, again worried about the impact of the Erie Canal and the B&O RR, the Pennsylvania Railroad Company started construction almost immediately and followed the same general route as the Main Line from Harrisburg to Hollidaysburg. The Pennsylvania RR followed the Juniata River waterway along its southern bank westerly through Waynesburgh and crossed over the river to Birmingham. From there it proceeded west to front range and into Hollidaysburg. (Eventually a new railroad town called Altoona would be built next to Hollidaysburg and the new Pennsylvania RR shops.) Again, railroad engineers followed the lowest elevation grades and the waterways upstream to prevent unnecessary and costly cut and fills. The Pennsylvania Railroad, at times called the Pennsylvania "Central" Railway, would be only the fourth railroad to cross the Appalachians. The first had been the Portage RR, followed by the rival B&O RR in Maryland in the mid-1840s. But, the Pennsylvania RR was much different than the Portage. First, it was a privately owned and operated railway and only was held responsible to its shareholders, not the citizens of the Common-wealth. So, taxpayers could not gripe to the Board of Canal Commissioners or other elected officials in Harrisburg about slow service and expensive freight cost. Second, it was initially designed to be a large-scale, long-distance railroad similar to the Pennsylvania Main Line Canal System linking Philadelphia to Pittsburgh. The difference was it would utilize only one form of motive power—locomotives. Third, it operated "for profit" and would compete with other routes for service. Fourth, it was to be an all-weather and an all-time railroad. The Pennsylvania RR would operate day and night and even in the cold winter months when the canals were frozen—probably its most important attribute. Fifth, it was the select railroad of the eastern political powers in the state. The B&O RR had a charter to operate in the state of Pennsylvania in 1846 and was in nearby Cumberland, Maryland by 1843. It was ready in the late 1840s to venture north toward Pittsburgh and link that city to Baltimore instead of Philadelphia. That is when the brakes were applied by the Commonwealth of Pennsylvania, and the B&O RR charter to operate in the Commonwealth as a corporation was "conveni-ently" allowed to expire in 1848 and was not renewed.

These main advantages and others such as modern locomo-tives and equipment, and the installation of the telegraph for in-stant communication, made the Pennsylvania RR the strongest rival ever for traffic in the state. Now the competition for western traffic was not confined to canals in New York and Maryland but came from within Pennsylvania itself.

The Conflict at Hand

The Humphreys saw this dilemma between the Main Line and the upstart instate railroad too. They saw the C&O Canal in Cumberland, the B&O RR near the Ohio River, and the Erie Canal widening and deepening its canal basin for additional traffic. In

1850, the Humphreys family's jobs, contracts, Summit Hotel, and Riffel & Humphreys were right in the middle of the convergence of the Pennsylvania RR and the old tired Portage RR. Their entire livelihood was based on the Portage and the people and patrons who lived near it at the Summit. Rowland lived next to Plane No. 5 and supplied the railroad with horsepower and hauling services. At that time, the Portage was hauling over 200,000 tons of freight annually, up from 127,000 tons in 1845.[5] The hauling contracts on the Portage were no small potatoes. Therefore, a great deal was at stake for Rowland and his sons.

The rail season of 1850 probably saw the largest number of Humphreys working on the Portage at any one time. They were Rowland, John, David, Thomas, James — and the Riffles too. In 1850, John Humphreys was a Portage engineer again for the first time since 1846, this time at Incline No. 4. His brother David was promoted to engineer from assistant engineer at that time, and worked with his brother Thomas, a fireman and assistant engineer, at Plane No. 8 in 1849 and 1850. They also worked at other various inclines including Nos. 2, 4, 8, 10.[6] Besides John, David worked on the Portage the second longest.[7] Thomas Humphreys worked at different jobs and locations during his short run with the Portage Railroad during 1849 and 1850. He lived in Summitville in 1850 with his parents, as David had during the late 1840s. Young James Humphreys may have been a driver for his father by 1849 and made coal deliveries to the engine houses in the early 1850s.

J. Edgar Thomson and the "Other" Railroad

Some saw the Portage and its many workers as part of the overall Main Line problem: "The planes gave employment to a large number of men, all of whom were more or less important in advancing the partisan interest of the party in power, and in consequence, the proposition to 'avoid the planes' met with sufficient opposition from that quarter to cause those in power to advise the postponement of the question to the uncertain future and to shade official opinions with the tintings of disapproval."[8]

The construction of the Horseshoe Curve in the early 1850s, by the Pennsylvania Railroad Company. The effort to construct this engineering project was amazing by any standard.

Sugar Run Gap was also used by the Pennsylvania Railroad Company to build its first railroad over the mountain in the early 1850s. This photo was taken just west of the famous "Horseshoe Curve" on the railroad's way to the tunnels at Gallitzin. The railroad route can still be seen in the upper right portion of the photo across from U.S. Route 22.

The Horseshoe Curve in the 1850s. A four-hundred-mile route from Philadelphia to Pittsburgh spelled the end to the state-owned Portage RR.

By September 1850, the four-year-old Pennsylvania RR had enough capital and manpower to lay track from Harrisburg all the way to the Mountain House in Hollidaysburg, a distance of one hundred miles. On October 1, it linked up to the Portage Depot at Duncansville, just a short distance west of Hollidaysburg. But the Pennsylvania RR had the same engineering problem as the Portage had in 1832. It had to cross over the "hilly section" too — then to Johnstown and eventually Pittsburgh. This time crossing had been well thought out by true railroad engineers. The Pennsylvania RR decided to cross over the mountain at Sugar Gap, the gap located to the north and next to Blairs Gap. This monumental engineering feat was going to take some time with all the massive cuts and fills and blasting of the mountain face. It could take hundreds, if not thousands, of men years to complete. But it was a better location than Blairs Run Gap. This additional construction traffic from the Pennsylvania RR gave the Portage RR some much-needed time to survive. But, it would be a strange business relationship.

At Duncansville the Pennsylvania RR stopped construction of its own line in order to utilize the Portage tracts as the means to cross over the range (they were the same gauge), until its own tracks up the Sugar Run were complete, around the now famous Horseshoe Curve and through a new tunnel at Gallitzin. This arrangement would work as long as the state accepted the idea of rail-sharing. So instead of one railroad company over the mountain top every day, two were sharing the same tracks. This would be an uneasy marriage of convenience for both sides.

The Portage needed the business of the Pennsylvania RR on their tracks, and the Pennsylvania RR needed an existing way to Johnstown until its own tracks were completed, mostly on the eastern slope of Allegheny Mountain. Once past Cresson Springs (a mile from Summitville) the Pennsylvania RR had a downward western slope to Johnstown, paralleling the existing Portage route for the next 26 miles. From there it diverted from the canal route to Freeport and took a southern route to Pittsburgh through Greensburg. But it still needed the important state-owned and -operated rails east of the Summit.

The introduction of the Pennsylvania RR at Duncansville would not complement the Portage RR but would be its competition. It would be a competition between the two railroads for freight going east and passengers going west. But who would win this race; the older and experienced Portage who held the political clout and local patronage, or the upstart Pennsylvania Railroad, which still had to be built up one of the steepest mountains in the state? A letter to the Portage RR superintendent follows:

ENGINEER DEPARTMENT P.R.R. CO. }

HARRISBURG, NOV. 1st, 1850 }

DEAR SIR: I have received yours of the 16th. The difference between our case and yours is —

First. That we have a single track and must run one way at least to schedule or we would delay all of the trains on the road. So as to cause indescribable confusion.

Second. We run between two of the Commonwealth roads, and if we don't break connection with the Portage by waiting, we will with the Columbia road, and at the same time derange all our trains.

Of the two horns of the dilemma we have to choose the least. However, the season is now nearly over, and next year it seems to me that you will have to keep your planes going until midnight by two sets of hands. The business over the road, it appears to me, will require this arrangement. Yours truly,

J. EDGAR THOMSON,

Wm. S. Campbell, Esq., Supt. P. R. Road.[9]

A 1851 newspaper article about this same problem:
From the North Branch Democrat.

The Portage Railroad.

This road embraces a part of the main line of public improvements from Philadelphia to Pittsburg. The whole work has cost the State sixteen million dollars. The Portage Road is the railway connection from the terminus of the Canal on the east side of the Allegheny mountains, to the Canal on the west side, and constitutes ten planes. This State work yields a large revenue. The Central Railroad Company, chartered for the express purpose of contributing to the tonnage of the State improvements, and has largely increased the revenue of the State on the Columbia road, with which it connects, is now setting itself up as a rival to the State works, and among other things, has already taken an initiatory step towards avoiding the Columbia road, with the design of reaching Philadelphia by the way of the Lebanon valley and Reading, thus effectually destroying the utility of the Columbia road on the east.

On the west, this company is rapidly completing the road across the mountains without an inclined plane when the road is constructed to Pittsburg, it requires no argument to prove that it will monopolize all the carrying trade unless the inclined planes on the Portage road are avoided.

First, because neither passengers nor freight will be hazarded or delayed by inclined planes, when by the Central road they can be avoided and second, because transportation is much cheaper over a road without planes.

The annual cost of maintaining the planes on the Portage road, is from seventy to ninety-five thousand dollars. The stationary engines and machinery of the road is nearly worn out, and serious losses, by way of damages, are constantly occurring. The question that presents itself is simply this: Shall sixteen million of the public debt be thrown away, together with a large portion of the public revenue by which the interest on that debt is paid, and the whole surrendered to the Central Railroad Company; or shall the State make use of the means it would otherwise expend to keep up the Portage, for the purpose of avoiding these planes and thus compete successfully with the Central Railroad. Can there be any hesitation? Unless these planes are avoided the people must be burdened with increased taxation to supply the deficiency in the revenue, by being robbed of our main line of improvement.

The loan that was proposed for the Portage road, was chiefly to be reimbursed, by saving to the State, annually, the amount now required to keep it up.[10]

Cresson Springs

"The story goes that there was [and still is] a house at Cresson where the rain water off of one roof eventually ends up in the Atlantic Ocean, while the rain water off the other finds its way to the Mississippi Valley and the Gulf of Mexico."[11] Cresson Springs would be the place where the two railroads would eventually meet face to face and run side by side. Dr. R.M.S. Jackson proposed calling Cresson Springs "Rhododendron" for its beauty. By the early 1850s, however, the Pennsylvania RR made sure the new town would be named after Elliot Cresson, an early supporter of "their" railroad. Thus the name Cresson Springs was formally and forcefully adopted.

Construction of the Pennsylvania RR

The Pennsylvania RR had its own problems during the construction of its Western Division to Cresson Springs. It had to hack out a path through the virgin mountain timber and utilize huge cut and fill sections to create level beds around a curve called, of all things, "Horseshoe Curve," because of its design resembling a giant horseshoe. In February and again in May 1850, strikes by Irish laborers threatened to shut down the entire construction west of Johnstown, in nearby Westmoreland County. Violence and property damage occurred in June until some of the striking Irish workers were fired and evicted. The shortage of working capital and lack of understanding by an impatient and ever changing board of directors of this four-year-old company added to the slowdown—not too much different from the problems the Portage encountered during its first few years of construction and operation in the 1830s. Railroad construction through and around mountains was no easy task. Dealing with labor strikes, capital shortage, material shortage, and bad weather made the railroad construction a remarkable feat. Progress, although slow at times, did occur, and the Pennsylvania RR route to the Summit continued on both sides of the mountain:

> The PRR connected at Hollidaysburg in October 1850 with the state's Portage railroad. Unable to go around Allegheny mountain, the commonwealth built ten incline

planes, powered by steam winches, to life cars up the 2,570 feet and to ease them down to Johnstown. The thirty-six mile Portage, bracketed on either end by canals, was both inconvenient and slow; it had always been a bottleneck in the state works. Thomson and his board, however, were well aware of how much it was going to cost them and how much time it was going to take to push their railway over, around, or through the mountain. To save time they decided to construct the western division first and use the Portage temporarily to connect the two divisions until they could assault the mountain.

Use of the Portage immediately dumped a whole new set of problems into Thomson's already crowded lap. The PRR promised to be anything but a friendly adjunct to the state system; it threatened the jobs of everyone connected with the Main Line. Yet from the start Thomson needed the cooperation of the board of canal commissioners because his road depended upon the state's Philadelphia and Columbia Railroad for its connection with the state's port city and therefore had to jointly make schedules and set rates. Until the PRR reached the Portage, the commissioners were quite cooperative, loaning Thomson maps, delivering construction material, and allowing the PRR to construct its roadbed along and across the canal, sometimes destroying state buildings and other appurtenances. When Thomson began negotiating schedules for the Portage, however, he ran into trouble; the canal commissioners refused to operate the inclined planes at night, which meant passengers had to leave Philadelphia either at 4:00 A.M. or at 11:00 P.M. to avoid a wait at the base of the incline. When canal officials closed the Portage for the winter just a month after the PRR made its connection, Thomson protested privately. Publicly, however, he put the best face possible on the situation. He informed his shareholders that the closing was to make repairs and renewals that would allow the Portage to operate during subsequent winters.

...Yet when the canal board finally agreed in 1851 to keep the Portage open during the winter, it blithely raised its tolls over the inclined planes 33 percent. Thomson also noted that delivery times on the canal system averaged seven days while the B&O touted two-day service over the same distance, making him one of the earliest observers to recognize that the element of time was becoming critical in the competition for western trade. As the clash between the PRR and the canal commissioners ground endlessly on, he became even more anxious to push his construction over the mountains and across the western division.[12]

As soon as the Pennsylvania RR construction crews were close enough to Summitville, merchant John Humphreys was wise enough to see a chance to make lemonade out of lemons. He sold supplies to the Pennsylvania RR work camps on both sides of the mountain. If you can't beat 'em—join 'em! A newspaper article written the next winter stated:

The Portage Railroad.

It is gratifying to be able to state that this road continues in successful operation notwithstanding the severe freezing weather of the past few days. This is the first winter that the attempt has been made to keep the road open, and the present efficient board of Canal Commissioners deserve great praise for the interest they have manifested, and the repairs they have caused to be made, in order to effect so desirable result. The danger of the water freezing in the water-pipes, cisterns, &c., has always been supposed to be unavoidable, but judging from the careful preparations made by the Supervisor, and from the fact that everything is progressing smoothly and satisfactory, we are confident that the road can be used during the entire winter season.[13]

"In the winter of 1851–52 the Pennsylvania Railroad Company having purchased from the Commonwealth its passenger cars, passenger trains were for the first time moved over the road at night. While the Old Portage was in full use with its system of planes, its operating involved the necessity of changing power 33 times in 36 miles. To move a section boat over the road from the basin at Johnstown to Hollidaysburg involved calling into requisition 12 stationary engines, 12 different teams of horses, and 9 locomotives. The minimum number of men to handle this was 12 engineers and 12 firemen at the stationary engines, 9 engineers and 9 firemen for the locomotives, and 12 drivers of the teams—making 54 persons in all."[14]

Meanwhile, on December 10, 1852, a Pennsylvania RR train had reached Pittsburgh all the way from Philadelphia using the Portage and other railroads. Despite all difficulties the great project was done and the link was complete. The Pennsylvania RR had become the all-weather all-time route that many had dreamed of and others dreaded, such as the Portage and canal men on the Main Line. It would mean the end of "their" railroad and the end of their secure jobs in a matter of just a few years. But the competition still had to finish their track around the Horseshoe Curve and through the Gallitzin Tunnel to make it all Pennsylvania RR route. It was completed just in time. To the south in Virginia, the B&O RR had just completed their line from Cumberland, Maryland, to Wheeling, Virginia, along the Ohio River, on Christmas Day. Like the Pennsylvania RR it was an all-weather route that avoided canals or transfers. It seemed both railroads grabbed the same western prize in the same month of the same year.

John Humphreys and his wife continued to raise an even larger family during these troubled times of the early 1850s. His first child, John W. Humphreys, was followed by Edward R.(iffle) Humphreys in 1849, James R.(iffle) Humphreys about 1851, Hannah Humphreys about 1853/55, and Thomas A. Humphreys in January 1859. Thomas A. was named after his late uncle Thomas who died in Iowa of cholera in 1852. Hannah was the namesake of John Humphreys' sister who had also died young. All the children except John W. were probably born in Summitville Borough. James and Hannah died during the Portage years. The completion of the Pennsylvania RR to Cresson Springs was a turning point for all the Humphreys, but not as much as the untimely death of their father, Rowland, in 1852.

Chapter Ten
Death in the Staple Bend Tunnel

"Foot of Five"

By 1852 Rowland Humphreys had become a successful businessman, gentleman farmer, and Democratic political supporter in Cambria County. He was 55 years old. He and his wife, Catherine, had raised 11 children, 7 into adulthood. Rowland had served in the local militia in the 1830s as a captain. Three sons had done their patriotic duty and fought in the Mexican War; one was killed, and two came back as local heroes. Four sons had worked for the Portage. Rowland owned a 168-acre sheep farm in Cambria Township and sold the wool. He and his wife lived next to Ignacous Adams, the founder of the area, and their "magic springs." On September 9, 1851, Portage contractor and farmer Rowland Humphreys listed his address as "Foot No. 5" APRR, Washington Twp., in the Summit Mansion Hotel registration book.[1] It was one of a few entries he made in this rare book. Foot of Five was located at the foot of Incline No. 5, just about a mile from Summitville. He had lived there with his family for several years and conducted his contractor services there for the Portage. He had Portage contracts for hauling cars near plane No. 5 where he lived from the 1830s up to May 1850, a time when horses were still in use. "Fifty cents per day per horse, fifty cents per day per driver, 4 horses, 1 driver, $67.50 for the month of May."[2] The Portage RR, once a dream, had provided him with everything an immigrant could have wanted: steady employment, land, a bright future for his able sons. Then tragedy would strike.

On Saturday afternoon, June 12, 1852, Rowland Humphreys was killed in an accident on the Portage RR in the Staple Bend

Tunnel on his way to his home. Following is the newspaper article describing his accident:

Accidents.

On Saturday last more accidents occurred up on the Portage Railroad than during any one day since its construction. It was a day long to b(e) remembered in sadness and grief by many of our citizens and those immediately interested it was a day fraught with sorrow and tribulation.

One of our oldest and most respected citizens, Capt. ROLAND HUMPHREYS, while passing through the tunnel, four miles east of Johnstown, on Saturday afternoon, was caught between the section of a boat and the tunnel wall and was instantly crushed to death. His unfortunate situation was noticed by the driver of the team, and every effort was made to extricate him ere the vital spark of life had fled, but without avail. A part of the boat truck had to be cut away ere he could be taken out, so firmly was his body wedged in between the wall and the boat. The deceased was well and favorably known to all the citizens of our county, as also to many in the State, and by his loss society is deprived of one of its brightest ornaments, his family of a kind, humane, and well-beloved father. He was born in Wales, March 10, 1795, and came to this country while a young man, where by honest industry and untiring perseverance he established for himself an unblemished reputation, made a comfortable home, and maintained a large family of children. For a number of years he commanded a volunteer company in this county, "The Invincibles," and at the breaking out of the Mexican War, the patriotism of the father still slumbering in the bosoms of his sons, three of them volunteered for the Mexican campaign and served with honor and distinction in that war. One son was killed during the assault on the castle of Chapultepec while doing battle for his country's rights. The other two returned home at the close of the war and reside in our midst.[3]

Who would have thought that his untimely death would be due to an accident on the Portage of all things? The very fact that two generations of the family were involved for nearly 20 years was a strange twist of fate. Everyone knew the dangers of a railroad, but this was Rowland Humphreys. It is believed that Rowland was the second person to have been killed in the Staple Bend Tunnel in its 20 plus years of operation. A year before another man was killed in the tunnel while intoxicated. According to other Portage records, no one had been killed during the construction of the Staple Bend Tunnel. The freak accident in 1852 involving a canal boat in the tunnel was unbelievable. Unfortunately too late for Rowland, the practice of hauling canal boats on the flatbed cars was discontinued on the Portage two years later, in 1854.

Portage RR records do not indicate whether an official inquiry into the death of Rowland Humphreys was held by the Commonwealth. Accidents even to prominent and important people associated with the railroad were regarded as, well, "accidents." Blame was hard to affix when your everyday life was full of dangers. People simply moved on with their lives and got along as best they could.

Luck was not on the side of the Humphreys or Riffles on that day and night. The same night Rowland was killed a fire nearly destroyed the Summit Hotel. The registration book at the scorched Summit Hotel stated the following events of that awful day: *Saturday June 12, 1852, Capt. Roland Humphreys killed at A.P.R.R. Tunnel, Thomas Carroll's Leg taken off by Cars between 4 + 5, Michael Storm very badly injured on Plane 8, Stable of Mansion House burned down about 12 clk P.M.,* **Truly a day of Accidents.**[4]

Tragedy has a strange way of striking a third time in a very short period of time. A few days prior to Rowland's death in Pennsylvania, his son Thomas had died of that dreaded disease, cholera, in Iowa—the second sudden death in one month for the Humphreys family. The news did not reach Cambria County until June 28 as recorded in the Summit Hotel Ledger: *Monday Morning June 28, 1852, Thomas Humphreys Died of Cholera on 7th or 8th June, — Dubuque Iowa.*[5] A newspaper article a few days later stated

Staple Bend Tunnel, West Portal, First Railroad Tunnel Built in America, 1834. Photo taken August 2001.

Author's collection

(*Democrat and Sentinel*, July 8, 1852): "At Dubuque, on the 8th of June, of cholera, Thomas Humphreys, formerly of this county, aged about 22 years."[6] Thomas Humphreys was an engineer and fireman on the Planes Nos. 4, 8, 10 in the 1849 and 1850 seasons, before leaving for Iowa sometime later. A veteran of the Mexican War, he may have been going to Iowa or Kansas to see lands received as Bounty Land after his service in the army. Cholera, that dreaded water-borne disease, enemy of the canals and the Portage in Pennsylvania, was there in the Mississippi River next to Dubuque.

After his death, Rowland Humphreys was buried in Lloyds Cemetery just east of Ebensburg, the small town to where he had immigrated almost 40 years prior. He was buried in the family plot next to other family members who had died before their time, including his son William who was killed five years earlier in the Mexican War. Rowland's headstone, adorned with a weeping willow tree like his son's, reads the following, even to this day,

"Humphreys Rowland — born in Wales — died 1852 — Killed at the Allegheny Portage R. Road Tunnel."[7] His son Thomas who had died during that same month in Iowa was not brought back to Pennsylvania and was buried in a cholera cemetery in Dubuque. Rowland's daughter Hannah, age about 21 years, died the next year in March 1853. His wife, Catherine, would follow Rowland in 1858. Rowland's untimely death marked the beginning of a sad decade for the Humphreys. Wars, diseases, and accidents began to take their toll. Their American dream was quickly running out of steam — like the Old Portage itself.

Rowland's property was probated in Orphans Court a year later. In the description of the dozens of item accessed after his death to pay bills were a few of interest including his 168-acre farm in Cambria Township, valued at $2,520.00, and the Summitville Lot No. 6 with two houses at $200.00, 2,000 lbs. of wool valued at $643.33, carriage and fixture at $37.00, cooking stove and fixture $36.00, bed and bedding at $20.00, cow and bell at $20.00, windmill at $15.00, a silver watch $10.00, kitchen furniture at $10.00, a buffalo robe for $4.00, 14 Welsh books, a Walker & Johnston's Dictionary, and a riffle gun.[8]

Chapter Eleven
The "New" Portage Railroad

The New Portage

The "New" Portage RR was an entirely new railroad. Unlike its predecessor, it did not have to stop at every incline and plane to change motive power. The idea of "avoiding the inclines" had been discussed for some time by the Board of Canal Commissioners, even as early as 1836. In retrospect, the whole idea of inclines and levels might have been somewhat premature, and at the time of construction some considered it insane — but it was built anyway. In 1832, something, anything, had to be built to compete against New York's and Maryland's railroads to save the reputation of the Portage. In January 1837, just three years after the New Portage RR's opening, representatives from Westmoreland, Indiana, Cambria, Huntingdon, Mifflin, and Juniata Counties held a meeting in Hollidaysburg to discuss the matter of avoiding the inclines, and resolutions were sent to the legislature in Harrisburg. In 1839, surveys were made for a new route without the incline planes; but that was about it. The few inclines used on the sister railroad, the Columbia RR, had been eliminated in 1840 for the very same reason — they were slow and antiquated. But no one in Cambria County wanted to close the inclines down on the Portage, with the dozens of men employed on all 10 inclines and planes for so long. After all, the inclines worked and besides no other railroad had even attempted the same feat as the Portage — cross the Alleghenies head on. Most of all, the railroad was pumping tens of thousands of dollars into the local Cambria and Huntingdon (Blair after 1846) Counties' economies.

In 1846, the Pennsylvania Railroad Company caught everyone's attention by becoming the Portage RR's first potential rival and future competitor in long-distance traffic. The Pennsylvania RR also sought to run a transportation line from Philadelphia to Pittsburgh. To the businessmen in Philadelphia the issue was not access to the West but one of speed. Because of this "competitor" a new Portage RR without inclines was strongly *reconsidered* by the Canal Board to avoid being destroyed by an all-weather railroad rival like the Pennsylvania RR. By 1851, five years had elapsed and nothing had been done by the Canal Commissioners to address what was becoming a very real problem; not even the awarding of a construction contract on the Summit to avoid the incline planes. In the five important years from 1846 to 1851, many things had occurred to hasten another quick decision as what to do with the old state line. First, the Pennsylvania RR Company had effectively lobbied the legislature in Harrisburg not to have the charter of the rival B&O RR, a Maryland-based company, renewed in 1848. This action basically put the B&O out of business in Pennsylvania before they could lay their first mile of track. This made Pittsburgh, the desired B&O destination to the Ohio River, accessible only to the Pennsylvania RR. Then Pennsylvania RR built their line all the way to Duncansville from Philadelphia, and to Johnstown from Pittsburgh, following the exact routes as the Main Line canals in some areas. Without the burden of the slow canals and the numerous cargo transfers on the Portage and its inclines, and the Columbia RR, the Pennsylvania RR was in a league of its own. It looked, smelled, and breathed as a real railroad should. In the early 1850s, the Pennsylvania RR was the next generation of railroading in America, one based on speed and service.

By 1851, the Portage RR, the proclaimed engineering wonder of its time, was becoming an expensive "white elephant." The railroad was worn-out including the stationary engines that were over 15 years old. Governor William Johnson (Whig) and the Commonwealth of Pennsylvania agreed that something had to be done, but instead of abandoning the system and the millions

of dollars that had been pumped into the railroad, it was improved. Oddly enough at this same time, a big dent in the Mississippi traffic was made when tobacco, and pork and pork products
were shipped east and not south through New Orleans.[1] The entire reason for the entire state-owned route in the first place. But
this "pork trot" from Cincinnati did not create enough revenue
to justify keeping the inclines open. In 1852 the decision was made
to take some form of action. By July 1852 contracts were made for
the New Portage roadway, avoiding the planes altogether and
hopefully the expense of the inclines. When completed, it would
travel straight through on the (now 45-mile) route in only four
hours and require only a single locomotive, a few men, and a few
stops to make it all happen. The new railroad had to be successful. In 1852, the rival B&O RR to the south was just miles away
from linking Baltimore to the Ohio River at Wheeling (instead of
Pittsburgh), and the Pennsylvania RR was right next door. But
its biggest disadvantage was that it was still a "linking" railroad
and not an end-to-end or ever-expanding railroad—an evolve-
ment other railroads had accomplished during the last 20 years.
The Portage RR did not serve two distinct destinations or long
distance destinations as the Pennsylvania RR and the B&O did,
nor was it going to Pittsburgh and Philadelphia without canal
transfers. In retrospect, this set size, fixed location, and use,
doomed it from the start in 1833; the inclines made it even worse
by 1852. To the taxpayers' disbelief the canal commissioners in
power wouldn't scream "Uncle!" quite so soon. However, for
the Commonwealth of Pennsylvania in 1852 it was an economic
death spiral.

Again, expenses on the 36-mile railroad were outpacing revenues, but now at an incredible rate. Even in the biggest revenue
years of 1850 to 1853, when the Portage grossed over a million
dollars ($1,011,691), it still lost a half million ($502,174) due to the
operating expenses and the additional new construction on the
New Portage, including an ambitious 1,600-foot tunnel in Gallitzin.[2]
A one-mile-long tunnel near the Summit had been proposed for
the Portage as early as 1829 by Engineer Moncure Robinson to

Lithograph "Crossing of the Allegheny, Pennsylvania Railroad," circa the 1850s.

Courtesy of the Railroad Museum of Pennsylvania (PHMC), Pennsylvania Historical and Museum Commission

save on tract mileage, but was dismissed by the Canal Board as a "luxury." What had been considered a luxury in 1829 was a real necessity in 1852. Other expensive changes included larger and stronger locomotives with four or even six driving wheels instead of two and new passenger cars. By 1849, passenger cars were starting to look like passenger cars and not just like stage coach models or cattle cars. The earlier "stage coach" models were introduced to tempt the new passengers to use the railroad by providing them with something that looked familiar, but they were small, uncomfortable and boring except for the unexpected "snake heads." The new cars were designed to prevent people from walking alongside them en route and were larger, smoother, and safer. Gone were the days of the iron strips on the wooden rails and the snake heads when solid iron rails were installed. But these added improvements led to more financial woes. In 1853, revenues for the Portage were $224,627, but gross expenses amounted to over half a million dollars ($507,508). This equated to a loss in one year alone of $282,881, the largest ever in one season.[3] Expense figures like that had never been seen before in the 20-year history of the railroad. To add to this mountain size headache the good old B&O RR, the Portage's southern state rival, finally reached the Ohio River through Wheeling, Virginia, in 1853. Then a second competitor, this one out of state, was in operation. Another reason for both the Portage and the Pennsylvania RR to complete their independent projects.

Regardless of the unfavorable numbers and the financial bleeding, the construction work on both competing railroads continued as the article below illustrates:

A Visit to the New Railroads.

A few days ago we visited the three sections (No. 16, 17 and 18) of Messrs. Michael Burke & Co., on the New Portage Road, and that of Messrs. M'Granns & Reilly, Section 104, on the Central Railroad. Messrs. Burke & Co's. section is situate on the western slope of the mountain, about one mile west of the Portage tunnel and one mile north of Summitville. This work comprises several heavy embankments and through cuts. The largest embankment is the heaviest work of the kind we have ever witnessed, being about one thousand feet long and over ninety feet high at its greatest height, and will contain, when completed, two hundred thousand cubic yards of earth. Standing upon its summit your eye overlooks the tall hemlocks which grow around its base, and one is astonished to think of the immense amount of labor necessary to complete so stupendous a bank of earth. About ninety hands are employed, and it is thought, the work will be completed by the 1st of January next. We attended a dance at one of the "shanties" on this section, where we had the pleasure of "tripping the light fantastic toe" with several of the fair daughters of the Emerald Isle. Here for the first time, did we witness the "old country folks" dancing their jigs, hornpipes, and other dances, to the shrill music of the pipe, until we fairly imagined our self to be in the land of their nativity. We never enjoyed a dance better, and never tripped it harder, and it was peculiarly gratifying that the evening's enjoyment passed away to the satisfaction and pleasure of all, nothing occurring to render it otherwise.

The Section of Messrs. M'Granns & Reilly, is situate immediately west of Allegheny tunnel, extending one mile and a quarter parallel and in close proximity to that of Messrs. Burke. On this section there are three fills and the same number of heavy through cuts. Our observation was principally confined to the "deep cut" near the tunnel, which is fifteen hundred feet long and over eighty feet in depth, out of which, when it is completed, there will have been taken over ninety thousand cubic yards of clay and rock, principally of the latter. Take it all in all this is the most extensive cut and much the largest section on the western division of the road. That a railroad *could* be made through such a mountain as is here, seems impossible, and yet the reality teaches us that in side of four months, the work will be ended, and but a short time afterward the scream of the iron-horse will be reverberating through "the bowels of the earth." The gentlemanly contractors have our thanks for their kind attention, and we hope ere long to give a more extended account of their operations than will be found in this imperfect sketch.[4]

In March 1854, the Allegheny Portage RR celebrated its 20th anniversary. It was not celebrated wth the normal bands, parades, canal fire, or speeches but was celebrated quietly. The future after 20 years was quite bleak. Just a month prior the reality of the full venture finally took root with this news from the Pennsylvania RR: "On February 15, 1854, the Pennsylvania Railroad withdrew their business from the road. This was a staggering blow to its friends and advocates, and in consequence, work progressed slowly during the season of 1854. The expectation of its completion, and at a cost within the appropriation of the Legislature, was not realized. This fact seems to have had its influence upon public opinion, which was rapidly crystallizing into the belief that the sale of the main line of the public works was a pressing necessity. That portion of the road, avoiding Planes Nos. 9 and 10, was opened April 23, 1855."[5] Revenues on the Portage in 1854

were down by 65 percent due to withdrawal of the Pennsylvania
RR traffic and their own open through line.

By early 1855, the new tracks of the Pennsylvania RR were
in place, bypassing the Portage with a direct non-stop route to
Pittsburgh.[6] By then, the Pennsylvania RR had its own tracks from
Philadelphia to Harrisburg to Pittsburgh for 247.8 consecutive
miles, 136 miles doubletracked.[7] The Pennsylvania RR had ex-
actly one hundred train stations from Philadelphia to Pittsburgh,
with Philadelphia as Station No. 1 and Pittsburgh at Station No.
100. Cresson was Station No. 66, and located 146 miles from Philadelphia and 101.8 miles from Pittsburgh by rail. Since train stations at Duncansville and Hollidaysburg were off the official
through route and a "spur" south of Altoona, they were given
letters instead of numbers. Duncansville was Station "M" and
Hollidaysburg was Station "K." Blairsville was also on a spur
line in Indiana County and was given the letter "L." No rhyme or
reason for the station letters "M," "K," or "L" was given.[8] (Years
later railroad signal towers of the Pennsylvania RR were given
two letters for identification. The tower in Cresson became "MO"
for no known reason.)

Not to be outdone, the "New" Portage opened its new routes
on July 1, 1855, bypassing Summitville and the Summit altogether
(including incline Planes Nos. 4, 5, 6, 7, and 8) with a direct route
from Cresson Springs to Gallitzin (actually Tunnel Hill) using a
new tunnel, and around the eastside of Allegheny Mountain. The
track then wound through "Mule Shoe Curve" just before Plane
No. 8 in Blairs Gap Run and on to Duncansville and Hollidaysburg.
This new tunnel for the new Portage RR, called Allegheny Tunnel, was near the Pennsylvania RR tunnel in Gallitzin. The Allegheny Tunnel was not quite as long as the Gallitzin Tunnel and
not completely finished inside when it opened for business in
July 1855. On opening day, Henry E. Hudson, engineer of the
locomotive "Pittsburg," was the first to use the new Portage route.
By then, over $2,000,000 had been spent on the new path and
upgrades.[9] But was it worth it?

The new Portage route was a giant semi-circle around the
Summit and away from the folks who lived there including the

Map of Cambria County, Pa., 1855

N

INDIANA
COUNTY

CAMBRIA   COUNTY

Carrolltown

Loretto

"Horseshoe
Curve"

Altoona

Ebensburg

Gallitzin

Munster

Summerville

Cresson

Hollidaysburg

Turnpike
Connection

Lilly

"Mule Shoe
Curve" Duncansville

Little
Juniata
River

Cassandra

Conemaugh   River

Portage

(Gap)

Conemaugh
Viaduct

Jefferson (Wilmore)

Newry

Conemaugh

Summerhill

South Fork

Johnstown

Staple Bend
Tunnel

BLAIR
COUNTY

SOMERSET COUNTY

BEDFORD COUNTY

- A. Portage RR Route
- Penn. RR Route
- Overland Turnpike
- Important Rivers

- Not to Scale

© Chris J. Lewie, 2001

Sugar Run Gap was used by the Portage RR in 1854 to build the "New" Portage RR and avoid all incline planes. The new route went around Allegheny Mountain and Summitville, under Gallitzin (actually Tunnel Hill), to Cresson. This photo was taken just outside "Mule Shoe Curve" near current U.S. Route 22. The old railroad route was used until 1981 by Conrail and can still be seen slicing across the left portion of the photo.

Humphreys and the Riffles. It meant that, after 20 years, no more trains would pass directly through Summitville. No more stops in front of the Summit Hotel or the merchant shops. No more passengers waving from their coaches. No more immigrants willing to buy breakfast, lunch, or dinner on the fly. It seemed as though the whole world of Summitville and the "old" Portage RR had stopped in that one day in July 1855. The new village of Cresson Springs, just a mile away, was now the railroad station on top of the mountain—for both railroads. But even this new route proved too little too late for the Portage for it was still tied to those damn slow canals. If it had only been built as a railroad for its entire 400-mile length (as envisioned in 1829), avoiding any and all canals, this would not have happened.

The New Portage had larger and stronger locomotives that could pull larger loads all the way through to Johnstown. Some locomotives even had four drivers and four leading wheels similar to the "American" type of the late 1850s. An account of the New Portage and those new locomotives: "While the Old Portage was in operation ten to twelve hours was required to transport a freight train or a section boat to Hollidaysburg, but the new Portage system only required four hours, and a day's work to run there and return to Johnstown, the round trip being eighty-two miles. There were no regular brakemen and the stops were made by the engineer, with the reverse lever, and by the fireman twisting the tank brake. After dusk the officials were not particular what the employees did with the engine, and frequently they would raise steam and start off to attend a country frolic, and leave the locomotive stand on the main track, without guard or a light, as no lamps or torches were provided for night work. On Sunday the engine would be taken out at the pleasure of the crew who would go where they desired. Even on week days, while hauling a train, the engine would stop anywhere to take up a weary traveler—man or woman, boy or girl, or a lot of either—and many a funeral cortege was put on the engine and tank and conveyed to its destination. No charge, and every one was made happy."[10]

Even in the twilight of the Portage RR there were lighter moments and good times along route, such as those mentioned above. That should be noted along with the seriousness of the work and the situation caused by the Pennsylvania RR setting up shop in Cresson in 1855. Families came together in times of need, as during the Mexican War, and when Rowland Humphreys was killed in the Staple Bend Tunnel. The people in Summitville relied on their faith in 1855; their future seemed uncertain with the changes occurring in Cresson.

Cost

The Pennsylvania RR charged 25 cents per mile to transport freight compared to the Portage's almost 30 cents per mile. It wasn't too difficult to determine which railroad to use to get to Johnstown or back to Hollidaysburg. The Portage dropped from a healthy $224,627 in 1853 to $78,025 in 1854, the same year the Pennsylvania RR withdrew their traffic.[11] In 1855, revenues were just $18,150, a 92 percent drop in revenues in just three years.

Expenses on the line soared with all the new equipment and up-grades! The Pennsylvania RR was getting all the traffic, all the people, and all the profits. It was time for the Commonwealth to admit defeat.

Foreseeing this disaster in 1854, the Portage and the entire Main Line System were put up for sale for $20 million even before the new Portage was complete. The Commonwealth, especially Governor William Bigler, had had enough even before the "New" Portage was finished, and then watched revenues dwindle afterwards. By 1855, and the opening of the New Portage RR, it had no takers even when reduced to $10 million to spur interest. That same year it lost $282,881. From 1850 to the end of 1857 the Portage lost over one million dollars. It was just too late to compete with the Pennsylvania RR. By now the Pennsylvania RR had a whopping 118 locomotives over 400 track miles, compared to the few dozen or so on the 41-mile Portage route.[12] The Commonwealth was ready to sell the Portage Railroad — new and old at this point. It was just a matter of time and how much could be recouped.

In the meantime, the Humphreys brothers, John and David, did their best to hang on until the bitter end. The Portage was all they knew and it still paid the bills in Summitville. The Humphreys brothers were also able to keep their jobs on the New Portage as engineers despite the railroad's need for few employees. Many other Portage men were let go after the inclines were closed in July 1855. As a consolation, there were a few other jobs assisting with the disassembly of portions of the "old" route for scrap iron. Ironically, those were workers employed to take apart their old way of life.

Both John and David were involved in the dismemberment of the same railroad on which they had worked for a decade. John worked as a foreman on the New Portage in November 1855. Although the Official Check Roll states "of Labor performed in making repairs on the Allegheny Portage Rail Road," it is assumed that John and six others (including two carpenters) were in fact disassembling it after the New Portage had bypassed the Summit in July.[13] This is the only time the Humphreys were ever listed as "making repairs" to the Portage. But after the old Portage had closed, any job was a good job. A total of 182½ man days were worked in November for an amount of $207.06 in wages. John worked 30 consecutive days for $1.50 per day overseeing the dismemberment of the rails.

The next month David Humphreys continued as foreman overseeing a few men from December 13 to January 5, 1856, 19 days of "Removing old Iron" (at $2.25 per day) at No. 4 and other locations. For some reason he gave his entire salary of $42.75 to a friend — William Mconnel.[14] David also worked nine days between December 1 to December 31, 1855 (at $2.25 per day) as an engineer on locomotives at Plane No. 4 on the New Portage near Lilly.

The next year, 1856, John, at the age of 33, became a "dispatcher" at the New Portage station in Cresson in 1856, making $2.00 per day. According to the Portage records he was the dispatcher from at least June 1 to December 31, 1856. The Portage RR station in Cresson was near the Pennsylvania RR station along Front Street. The Pennsylvania RR train station, No. 66, was located nearby at the foot of the Mountain House (which the Pennsylvania Railroad also owned), and near the old turnpike. It is highly unlikely that the two rival railroads would have shared the same train station in Cresson. But that would change in due time.

The Sale of the Main Line

For several months in 1857, letters and petitions circulated throughout the Commonwealth of Pennsylvania concerning the whole Main Line System, its operation, and its overall deficiencies. One "Letter" from Adams County summed up the way many citizens and fellow taxpayers felt about the entire Main Line System. Questions in the "Letters" included modes of keeping the account of expenses on the Main Line, disputed profits and disputed expenses, unreported expenses — the list was endless.[15] Just the accounting problems alone were enough to warrant serious investigations. It was becoming quite evident to statehouse leaders that something had to be done with the white elephant, and soon. In other words, the Main Line just had to go, the sooner the better!

The west portal of the Gallitzin Tunnel as it looked in 1857 at the end of the New Portage RR era.

Photo courtesy of the Railroaders Memorial Museum

The Gallitzin Tunnel was built by the Pennsylvania RR in 1853. The original tunnel is to the right and has been expanded. The second tunnel, at left, was built in 1905 and is currently unused. The "New" Portage tunnel, built at the same time as the Gallitzin Tunnel, was a few hundred feet to the south and is not shown in this photo taken in May 2000.

Chapter Twelve
The End of the Line!

It had had its day, and something better had taken its place;
and, instead of lasting for many generations,
the time of its existence was but about twenty-five years.

—Solomon W. Roberts, APRR Surveyor—Engineer 1831,
Speech read before the Historic Society of Pennsylvania,
April 8, 1878

The Auction

At an auction held on June 27, 1857, by the Commonwealth of Pennsylvania the entire Main Line System of Canals, including the New Portage RR, was sold. The only buyer for the Main Line was none other than the Pennsylvania RR. With a wink and a nod Mr. J. Edgar Thomson, President of the Pennsylvania RR, accepted the bid for $7.5 million. The $7.5 million selling price of the Main Line was about one-third its original asking price of $20 million in 1854, but the Commonwealth was just glad someone bought the lot of public works. Mr. Thomson was also the man who built the Horseshoe Curve and most of the track in and around the old and New Portage RR. No other man of his stature knew the system better than he. But Mr. Thomson and the Pennsylvania RR were also in a bind. By now the B&O RR had reached Parkersburg, Virginia, and was about to cross over to Ohio, or worse, lease track all the way to St. Louis. The B&O also expanded its territory west as any decent railroad would have in the 1850s. It was strictly business. The Pennsylvania RR needed the additional track for access in and out of the Juniata Valley, which seemed at times to put a choke hold on the entire Pennsylvania

RR system in bad weather and during routine maintenance. When
the Gallitzin Tunnels or Horseshoe Curve were closed so was the
access to the West. The closure would then bottleneck on both
sides.

The Pennsylvania RR took formal control of the Portage RR
on August 1, 1857, and operated it for only three more months.
Sadly, the New Portage RR with all its new tracks, tunnels, culverts, cut-and-fills, bypasses, and good intentions was discontinued on November 1, 1857. To the new owners, the railroad's
operation and maintenance was too costly. The closing of the
brandnew 1,620-foot New Portage tunnel, "Allegheny," which
had been built at Tunnel Hill and opened just two years prior
was also closed. The only thing needed was the track section east
of the tunnels. The final closing of the Portage RR marked the
end of the Commonwealth's big dream. The following is one of
the last pay receipts ever drawn up by James Bryden, supervisor
on the Portage Railroad:

> **Commonwealth of Pennsylvania**
>   **To John Humphreys**   DR.
> For service rendered as Witness + Expenses, Horse Hire,
> Mileage from Summit to Hollidaysburg (10 miles) In care of
> damages between the Commonwealth + Robert Lemon.
>   5.20
> Rec. Nov. 14, 1857 of James Bryden State Supt. of A.P.R.R.
> Here relay Twenty cents in full of the above — Bill
>   *John Humphreys*
> I do certify that the above Bill is correct and that I called Mr.
> Humphreys in behalf of the Commonwealth.
>   *James Bryden*[1]

How fitting that one of the last pay receipts would be to
none other than John Humphreys. The Humphreys family was
there when the Portage Railroad opened in 1834, helped with the
operation and maintenance for over 20 years, disassembled it in
1855 and 56, and closed it in 1857. In 1858, the Pennsylvania RR
began removing the new iron rails that had been laid in 1853 by

the Commonwealth and shipped them west to the Pittsburgh, Fort Wayne & Chicago Railroad. They were used in the extension of the line from Plymouth to Chicago. Some of the stone blocks, including the sleepers, were removed and used in Altoona to build the new shops for the Pennsylvania RR. It also acquired about 72 locomotives, mostly from the Columbia RR, and a few from the Portage RR. Acquired from state: 58 with 4 drivers weighing from 38,000 to 67,200 pounds; 8 with 6 drivers, whose weight is not indicated in the inventory; 3 Baldwin and 3 William Norris engines—number of drivers and weight not indicated in the inventory.[2]

The locomotives and freight cars were dispatched throughout the Pennsylvania RR system after 1857. By now the Pennsylvania RR was looking at a much bigger picture that included stretching all the way to Cincinnati and the Ohio River to capture once again that important western trade market. (It would later take the final step and build all the way to St. Louis and the great Mississippi River.) The same idea first emerged in Philadelphia in 1825 in reaction to the Erie Canal. The additional Portage RR and Columbia RR locomotives and cars would help to accomplish that 30-year-old dream. Some locomotives, like the "Wheatland" from the Columbia, were later rebuilt and "beefed up" and used for many additional years afterward. (In 1860, it transported H.R.H. the Prince of Wales [later King Edward VII] from Pittsburgh to Philadelphia via Cresson.) The older locomotives, as the "Wheatland," were issued three-digit numbers and were required to drop their unique names like "Backwoodsman," "Mountaineer," "Bush Hill," "Benjamin Franklin," and "United States" due to the hundreds of locomotives that then existed and the complex paperwork associated with maintaining them.[3] The renumbering of the many locomotives was more "corporate" and businesslike.

On July 18, 1858, the first Pennsylvania RR train rode entirely on Pennsylvania RR tracks from Philadelphia to Pittsburgh, about 450 miles in about 13 to 17 hours, instead of few days. Twenty-five years prior it would have taken several long bumpy weeks to cover the same rugged, uneven, and rough local roads. Railroads by 1858 in America could cross states like Pennsylvania in a single day's time. Passengers could even sleep on board during the trip. Some visionaries saw railroads on the verge of crossing the other continental divide way out west and reaching the Pacific Ocean 2,500 miles away. The engineering and building of a railroad was one thing, running it another, operating it at a profit still another. The Commonwealth of Pennsylvania learned all three lessons over a 25-year span.

In 1859, the Pennsylvania Main Line Canal Commission was disbanded, ending the entire state-sponsored canal/railroad endeavor. Pennsylvania's efforts were hampered by starting late in the great canal race, and its railroad was the first to shut down. Although plagued with engineering and logistical problems from the start, the railroad accomplished what it had set out to do in 1826: open a way through the mountains. It would be only a short time later when the other canals, both public and private, in Pennsylvania would also be disbanded, shut down, and some sold to companies like the successful Pennsylvania RR for new railroad lines. In doing so by 1860, the Pennsylvania RR stated revenues of five million dollars. By 1865, revenues had soared to $19.5 million.[4] A few decades later the Pennsylvania RR became the largest employer in the state and the largest consumer of both steel and coal in the Commonwealth. The business growth of railroading was incredible in the 1800s.

Its Place in History

Some rail historians claim the Allegheny Portage Railroad was a waste of state funds, totally unnecessary, overly expensive, and even a political disaster from its inception. I am inclined to believe that the Old Portage must be remembered for its engineering achievement and that it succeeded its primary purpose of opening up the economic resources from the Midwest to Pennsylvania. According to the 1860 *American Railroad Journal (ARJ)* report, the Old Portage RR financially broke even between 1834 and 1850, when comparing expenses to receipts. The New Portage RR just prolonged its life until the private sector, the Pennsylvania RR, could cross the mountain with its own railroad with improved locomotives a few years later. But remember, the Allegheny Portage RR helped to kickstart the industrial revolution and the great age of steam power. It was built and operated until better railroad technology was available for an all-time and all-weather railroad. This technology, along with will power, fostered the famous Horseshoe Curve and the Gallitzin Tunnels, which 150 years later are still in operation. The industrial age of steam power started in the Juniata Valley and the Allegheny Highlands, then shifted to Johnstown and eventually Pittsburgh. Everyone remembers Pittsburgh for its steel, some even Johnstown for coal, but not everyone remembers where it all started 50 years before with the canals, the incline planes, and the Cambrians. Railroading in the mountains was not an exact science. It evolved with a series of small, incremental steps, successes, failures, deaths, and leaps of faith until one day the whole thing worked and railroading, like engineering and civil planning, became somewhat of a science. New technology has the tendency to do that. It evolves. There are always construction overruns, poor designs, slow service, bad choices, less than spectacular returns, floods, economic panics, wars, and ongoing maintenance that are followed by government subsidies, buy-outs, foreclosures, and rebirths. Sound familiar?

The Portage did not survive long in terms of length of service of a railroad, and it really did not siphon the large amount of western traffic as anticipated. Its attempt to rival the Erie Canal failed. But it did serve its commercial purpose of providing a linkage to two geographic regions where there had been none. It linked Philadelphia to Pittsburgh for the first time in travel time measured by days not weeks. It did so in times of peace and war, and in good times and economic collapse. Most of all it moved dreams.

It helped move thousands of European immigrants to their new homes in the heartland of America. It brought commerce from the Ohio Valley to Philadelphia. It moved war supplies in 1847 to the Gulf of Mexico and adventurous easterners to the gold fields in California in 1849. In part it helped foster the idea of Manifest Destiny or the expansion of the West to the great

Pacific Ocean where and when it was needed. The Portage RR accomplished all that as a large public works program that stretched for four hundred miles. A goal of democratic society. Some projects of this size have greater goals and provide greater benefits than just a construction project or works program. Others come at the right place and at the right time.

By closing the Portage RR down in November 1857, Pennsylvania closed one of the greatest chapters in early American railroad history. How ironic, that the Pennsylvania RR that built next to it, competed against it, and eventually owned it, would become the next great chapter in American railroad history. An evolution took place between the first and the second generation of Pennsylvania and American railroading — one that progressed and evolved into the 20th, and now the 21st century. This progress was envisioned back in 1834 when the Alleghenies were crossed by man and machine for the first time.

For the Humphreys the closing of the Portage RR was a sad ending to a great little mountain railroad. A way of life and prosperity had developed around it affecting three generations by 1857. But its closing did not dampen their enthusiasm toward railroads or railroading. After the closing of the Portage came the mighty Pennsylvania RR. For some this meant jobs, good jobs, high-paying jobs, in nearby Cresson, Johnstown, Pittsburgh, and Tyrone. For the next generation of Humphreys like John's son John W. the "Pennsy RR," as it was called, meant a future association with the steam locomotives that had incredible speed and power. Danger was still the norm for railroaders like this family, but that did not seem to stop them. The family moved on from one railroad to another without missing a beat. Well, at least some family members did.

Epilogue

I've been working on the railroad
All the livelong day,
I've been working on the railroad
To pass the time away.
Don't you hear the whistle blowing?
Rise up so early in the morn.
Don't you hear the captain shouting,
"Dinah blow your horn."

I've Been Working on the Railroad
Anonymous

Two generations of the Humphreys family did quite well working for both the Old and the New Portage RR in some capacity as contractors, merchants, engineers, firemen, drivers, state agent, and finally dispatch. The following is what is known about the major players in the Portage Railroad after 1857:

John Humphreys may have joined the Pennsylvania RR in the late 1850s in Cresson, like his bother David and friend Henry Hudson. After his wife of only 13 years died in January 1859, things changed again for John. In 1860 he was a merchant again in Summitville, and by 1862 he became an officer in the 54th Pennsylvania Volunteer Infantry in the Civil War guarding the B&O RR lines (their old competitor) against rebel raids near Hancock, Maryland. When his three-year enlistment was up in 1865, he returned to Summitville at the time when his first son, John "William," joined the Pennsylvania RR. John Humphreys had the distinction of working on the Portage RR, fighting in the Mexican War, and again in the Civil War without being seriously injured.

He was very lucky indeed and fate was on his side. Any one of the three ventures could have been fatal and had proved to be to someone close to him. William died in the Mexican War, Thomas of cholera, and his father in the Staple Bend Tunnel.

After John Humphreys returned from the war in 1865, he returned to the Summit and lived there for about a year. In 1866, he moved to East Conemaugh Borough (next to Johnstown) near his brother David and his family. Hard times were about to set in. He held odd jobs as laborer and may have been a coal miner in the local bituminous coal mines. Later he sold his property in Summitville and became a common laborer. In 1877 he moved again, this time to Pittsburgh, to be with his son William, his wife, and new grandson, Gordon. By 1884 he worked as a watchman at the Black Diamond Steel Works until about 1892 when he could no longer work and collected an army pension. In 1898 he died at his home on Mulberry Street. His body was returned to Cambria County and buried at Headrick's Cemetery just outside of Johnstown, in a plot next to his sister Mary (Humphreys) Wike, and near his brother David, who had died in 1885. Unfortunately, one hundred years of weathering have wiped out the inscription on John's marble headstone, but not his life. He was quite a man of his generation and survived the two wars, cholera, "snake heads," and economic misfortune.

John's first son, John "William" Humphreys, was born and raised near the Portage and joined the Pennsylvania RR as a fireman about 1865 at the end of the Civil War. After the Civil War, he may have moved to Johnstown and East Conemaugh Borough. While in East Conemaugh he lived next to his uncle David who also worked on the Pennsylvania RR. In 1870, William moved to Pittsburgh and worked as an engineer on freight trains and later passenger lines like the "Derry Express" until 1912. His career lasted 47 years. His decision to join the Pennsylvania in 1865 provided his family and grandchildren with job security that lasted until 1939. Like his father, William loved steam locomotives and the mystique surrounding them.

Not much is known of William's two younger brothers, Thomas and Edward. What is known is that Ed like his brother

William was raised Catholic, and Thomas a Protestant. Also, the two brothers carried on the heritage of working the rails. Thomas was a conductor on the Pennsylvania RR, while Ed was an engineer on the Pennsylvania & NW RR in Bellwood. Ed and Thomas later married and had three daughters each, thus ending the Humphreys namesake line at the time. Not much was known of the life of the Humphreys daughters.

John's Brothers from the Portage Years

David Humphreys, after the Portage years, moved to Blair County (possibly Altoona), then back to Cambria County to the Johnstown area (East Conemaugh Borough) about 1866. There he worked as an engineer on the Pennsylvania RR for many more years. He and his wife, Margaret M. (Lane) Humphreys, had at least four children: Charles R., Harry B., Emma J., and Clara. David worked on the Pennsylvania RR until his death in 1885, at the age of 58. He was one of the few to work directly for both the Portage RR and the Pennsylvania RR, and the only one documented of this family. He and his family are buried in Headrick's Cemetery north of Johnstown. Unlike his brother John, David lived almost his entire life in Cambria County. His sons Charles and Harry both were locomotive engineers on the Pennsy RR. It was really in the blood by now!

James Humphreys, the youngest of the brothers, may have been a driver on the Portage about 1850, and may have stayed in Cambria County after the Portage years. Not much is known about him afterwards. He may have died in 1871 but records are not clear. What is known is that during the U.S. census in 1870 no Humphreys, not even the small children and grandchildren, were listed in Summitville or Washington Township. They all had moved away to places like Johnstown and Pittsburgh, but they never forgot their roots, and always seemed to come back to their uncles' Summit Mansion Hotel for special occasions, like Christmas, in the 1860s.

James M. Riffle owned and operated the Summit Mansion Hotel for 20 years until his death in 1872. He was the only one of the two families who stayed after 1870. Some of the Riffles family stayed in the Altoona area where descendants are found even to this day.

The Summit Mansion Hotel

After the Portage Railroad left and the Pennsylvania Railroad took over, the Summit Hotel did not decline in character or business as projected by some in the area. The population of Summitville had dropped from 406 people in 1850 to just 153 in 1860 (a decrease of 62.3 percent). But some may have moved to nearby Cresson. The character of the area was changing again.

The hotel received travelers from the newly built Pennsylvania RR station in Cresson Springs, located one mile to the northwest and below the Summit. The PRR also operated its own hotel in Cresson. It had dismantled and moved the Mountain House from Hollidaysburg to Cresson for the same reason: to entertain guests in the clear mountain air. Later, all east and west bound trains on the Western Division of the PRR line would stop at Cresson and see the hotels and drink the cool mountain water. The Summit Hotel received added business during the Civil War as troop trains would stop in Cresson from Pittsburgh and the West as they traveled to Washington and the Virginia campaigns. An article from 1872:

> **A REUNION OF THE OLD PORTAGE RAIL ROAD MEN.** — At a meeting of those who were engaged upon the State improvements, known as the Old Portage Railroad and Pennsylvania Canal, before their abandonment, says the Johnstown *Daily Voice*, held at Summit, Pa., Friday, July 13, an organization was effected and the following officers elected: President-John Quayle; Vice-Presidents-Peter Dougherty and James M'Closkey; Recording Secretaries-Wm. M'Connell and J. E. Storm; Corresponding Secretary-T. C. Myers. After an explanation of the object of the meeting. it was
>
> *Resolved*, That we do have a second re-union of those who were employed upon the line of State improvements,

at the "Summit House," Summit, Pa., on Wednesday, October 2d, 1872.

Resolved, That appropriate committees be appointed to carry the first resolution into effect.

In pursuance of the second resolution, the following committees were appointed:

Corresponding Committee — Wm M'Connell, J. E. Storm, John Sharbaugh, Peter Dougherty and **John Riffle**, Summit; John Campbell and James Maloy, Johnstown; Charles McManamy, Loretto; Joseph Parks, East Conemaugh; John Major, Pittsburgh; John Ross, McVeightown; Jesse Crawford, Martha Furnace; ex-Mayor Potts, Powell Sharp and **George Riffle**, Altoona.

Committee of Arrangements — Henry Hughes, James W. Condon, William M'Connell, J. E. Storm and Dan Criste.

Committee on Music — C. Reich, Summit; Jno. Black, Pittsburgh; **David Humphreys**, East Conemaugh.

Committee on Orators — John Sharbaugh, Henry Cassidy, W. W. Wike.

Committee on Reception — Jos. M'Closkey, Matthew Black, Isaac Wike, John M'Closky, Richard Trotter, Col. John A. Lemon.

On motion, the meeting adjourned, to meet at the call of the President.

Wm. M'Connell }
J. E. Storm }   Secretaries.[1]

Also, a similar version from the *Johnstown Daily Voice* was found glued in the Summit Mansion House Registration Book.

This Old Portage Railroad Men meeting on October 2, 1872, probably became the "Grand Ball of the Engineers" held by the Pennsylvania RR at the Summit House on October 7, 1874.[2] It is uncertain if they held this railroad reception every year. Many reunions of the old Portage men were held at the Summit during the 1870s, 1880s and into the 1890s. The last known reunion of the Old Portage RR was held on August 8, 1891.

Ebensburg

Ebensburg, long left out of the railroad world, finally received railroad service in July 1862 from the "Ebensburg and Cresson Railroad Company" (with financial assistance from the Pennsylvania RR). That small 11-mile branch line from Cresson to Ebensburg, built for passenger and freight service, took three years to construct along the steep route. Freight hauling to Ebensburg included coal, lumber, and bark for tanning purposes. Ebensburg remains today a small cozy mountain community.

Allegheny Portage Railroad

The land around Plane No. 6 became a National Historic Site by an act of Congress in 1964 and is maintained by the National Park Service. Portions of Portage RR that have been restored include Plane No. 6, the engine house, and the adjacent Lemon House. The Historic Site stands as a reminder of the contribution to Pennsylvania's industrial and rail transportation past. In 1987, the American Society of Civil Engineers awarded the Allegheny Portage Railroad its designation as a "National Historic Civil Engineering Landmark."

The Pennsylvania Railroad

The Pennsylvania Railroad became one of the largest railroads in the country after 1860. At one time in the late 1800s it was the largest consumer of steel and coal in the entire state. By 1920, it had grown to 279,787 employees and a payroll of 362 million dollars. The Pennsylvania Railroad, called in later years the "Pennsy," *was* the industrial revolution in the Midwest. Decades later, in 1968, after its decline, it merged with New York Central RR to form Penn Central RR. In 1975, both merged into the government railroad system called Conrail. To this day the Pennsy RR still casts a long shadow on the Juniata Valley and has its own Railroad Workers Museum in Altoona.

The Horseshoe Curve

The Horseshoe Curve, after being part of the Pennsy RR for over one hundred years, was later transferred to Penn Central (later

The visitors center of the Allegheny Portage Railroad National Historic Site near Gallitzin, Pennsylvania. The Historic Site was established in 1964.

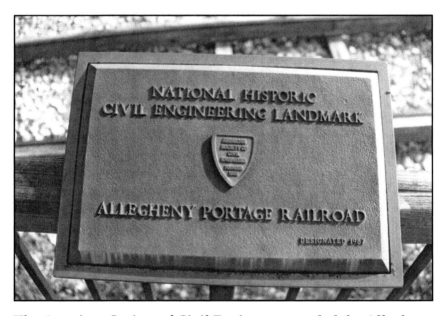

The American Society of Civil Engineers awarded the Allegheny Portage Railroad its designation as a "National Historic Civil Engineering Landmark" in 1987. The plaque is on display near the recreated Engine No. 6 at the APRR National Historic Site.

Conrail, and then Norfolk Southern). Located just west of Altoona it was designated by the federal government as a National Historic Landmark. The Curve is still in operation after nearly 150 years of everyday use, as are the nearby Gallitzin Tunnels.

Cresson/Gallitzin Area

The region would become famous years after the Portage Railroad era as the birthplace and childhood home of another famous man — Robert E. Peary. On May 6, 1856, Robert or "Bertie" E. Peary was born to Charles Nutter Peary and Mary (Wiley) Peary. His birthplace was located at the intersection of the old Turnpike and Loretto Plank Road in Cresson near the first Pennsylvania RR station.

After several previous unsuccessful attempts (especially in 1898), on April 6, 1909, Capt. Robert E. Peary, U.S. Navy, guide Matthew Henson, and a group of four Inuits made history as the first men to discover 90 degrees north latitude, commonly

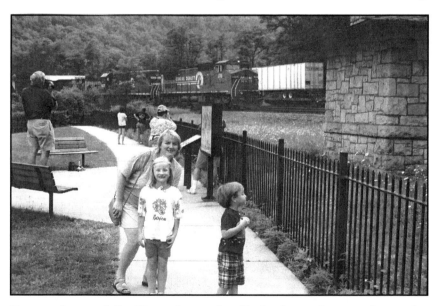

Descendants of the Humphreys family look at a locomotive at the famous Horseshoe Curve in July 1999. Pictured are the author's wife, Regina Lewie, *left,* and children, Kathryn Lewie, *center,* and Ryan Lewie, *right.* The Horseshoe Curve, built in 1854, is now a National Historic Landmark.

known as the North Pole.[3] Commander Robert E. Peary — the young lad from the Cresson/Gallitzin area — became world famous as the arctic explorer who led that successful expedition. A few years later he was promoted to admiral for his heroic services to his country. He died an international hero and explorer in 1920.

The Chesapeake & Ohio Canal

The C&O Canal never reached the Ohio River as intended. It stopped short at Cumberland, Maryland, in 1850 and used the Cumberland Road and B&O Railroad to Wheeling, West Virginia, and Pittsburgh. It was purchased in 1869 by railroad baron Collis Huntington, member of the Central Pacific Railroad, and one of the members of the "Big Four." The Big Four helped to finance and build the western portion of the transcontinental railroad from Council Bluffs, Iowa, to the Pacific Ocean, opening that same year of 1869. Similar to the Portage RR the Central Pacific RR was constructed by hand and tons of black powder — the last major project to be built in that manner before the advent of steam-powered equipment.

The C&O canal had its largest success during the 1870s hauling coal down the Potomac River toward Washington and Baltimore. The canal was devastated by the same May 1889 flood that hit Johnstown but reopened two years later and remained open until 1924, hauling mostly bulk items like coal to the Chesapeake Bay area. Large portions of the abandoned canal are now under the protection of the National Park Service as the C&O National Historic Park.

The Erie Canal

The Erie Canal saw its greatest years after the Civil War. Portions of the canal were widened and deepened to allow larger ships to pass and remain open after 175 years for service to this day. It was, and still is, truly an engineering marvel that has withstood the test of time.

New Tow Paths

All three major canal routes, the Erie Canal, the C&O Canal, and the Pennsylvania Main Line, became future pathways for the

Lock #52 of the Chesapeake & Ohio Canal near Hancock, Maryland. Canal boats would use four to six feet of water to maneuver. The tow path for the mules is to the right. The area is now under the protection of the National Park Service, known as the C&O Canal National Historic Park.

Interstate highway system of the late 20th century. Interstate 90 parallels the route of the Erie Canal in New York from Albany to Buffalo. Interstate 76/70, known as the Pennsylvania Turnpike, parallels the Pennsylvania Main Line from Philadelphia to Pittsburgh. And Interstate 70 and portions of Interstate 68 follow closely portions of the C&O Canal and the Potomac River in Maryland. It appears that the three original canal routes, destined for the riches of the heartland in the early 19th century, built through or around the Alleghenies, were not so poorly chosen after all!

Family Ties

To my ancestors, the Humphreys and the Riffles, the Allegheny Portage Railroad years seem like just a distant memory in a century full of incredible railroading activity. However, I believe that the early years on the Portage from the 1830s to 1850s were the most exciting, dangerous, and daring of all. Over four generations later we were still courageously "riding the rails," and it all began with the incline planes and levels on top of the Allegheny Mountain—the mountain that at one time separated east from west.

Appendix A
Table of Inclines and Planes, 1834

	Length in feet	Elevation Overcome	Percent Grade
Plane No. 1	1,607.74	150.00	9.30
Plane No. 2	1,769.43	132.40	7.50
Plane No. 3	1,480.25	130.50	8.80
Plane No. 4	2,194.93	187.86	8.50
Plane No. 5	2,628.60	201.64	7.70
Summit			
Plane No. 6	2,713.85	266.50	9.70
Plane No. 7	2,665.01	260.50	9.80
Plane No. 8	3,116.92	307.60	9.90
Plane No. 9	2,720.80	189.50	7.00
Plane No. 10	2,295.61	180.51	7.90

and the levels, as follows:

Ascending Eastward	Distance in Miles	Elevation Overcome	Percent Grade
Johnstown to Foot Plane 1	4.13	101.46	0.50
Head Plane 1 to Foot Plane 2	13.06	189.58	0.28
Head Plane 2 to Foot Plane 3	1.43	015.80	0.23
Head Plane 3 to Foot Plane 4	1.00	018.80	0.36
Head Plane 4 to Foot Plane 5	2.56	025.80	0.19
Head Plane 5 to Foot Plane 6	1.62	019.04	0.22
Descending			
Foot Plane 6 to Head Plane 7	0.15	Level	0.00
Foot Plane 7 to Head Plane 8	0.61	05.40	0.17
Foot Plane 8 to Head Plane 9	1.18	12.00	0.19
Foot Plane 9 to Head Plane 10	1.70	29.58	0.32
Foot Plane 10 to Hollidaysburg	3.72	146.71	0.75

Source: *The Evolution, Decadence and Abandonment of the Allegheny Portage Railroad*, by William Bender Wilson, 1897.

Appendix B
Financial Breakdown of Main Line Public Works

	Cost	Cost Per Mile
Canals:		
Canal from Columbia to Hollidaysburg, and canal from Johnstown to Pittsburgh	$ 8,327,889.01	$30,064.58
Railroads:		
RR from Philadelphia to Columbia	$ 4,204,969.96	$51,913.21
RR from Hollidaysburg to Johnstown*	$ 1,828,461.38	$50,790.59
Sub Total (399 miles)	$14,361,320.35	$35,993.28

Source: "Skew Arch Monument" near Plane No. 6 and Turnpike, erected 1928, south side of monument.

---

* $1.82 million for 36 miles

Appendix C
APRR Expenses and Profits 1834–1857

Year	Revenue	Expense	Difference
1834	$ —	$ 005,482	$ - 5,482
1835	97,740	098,744	- 1,004
1836	153,171	132,538	+ 20,633
1837	148,523	158,038	- 09,515
1838	153,069	148,648	+ 04,421
1839	151,330	141,857	+ 09,473
1840	167,266	267,333	- 100,067
1841	145,435	133,799	+ 11,636
1842	116,349	120,175	- 3,826
1843	175,476	159,920	+ 15,556
1844	169,603	208,137	- 38,534
1845	160,212	189,757	- 29,545
1846	200,342	130,321	+ 70,021
1847	232,587	160,290	+ 72,297
1848	219,143	220,181	- 01,038
1849	218,470	205,702	+ 12,768
1850	242,521	329,025	- 86,504
1851	234,532	341,325	- 106,793
1852	310,011	336,007	- 25,996
1853	224,627	507,508	- 282,881
1854	78,025	338,391	- 260,366
1855	18,150	256,458	- 238,308
1856	20,047	193,804	- 173,757
1857	11,982	82,850	- 70,868
TOTAL	$3,648,611	$4,866,290	$- 1,217,679
		10,044*	
		$4,876,334	$- 1,227,773

---

* Damages by sparks from locomotives

Source: *History of the Railroads and Canals of the United States of America, Exhibiting Their Progress, Cost, Revenues, Expenditures & Present Condition,* by Henry V. Poor, Esq., Editor of the "American Railroad Journal." 3 vols. — Vol. 1 (New York: John H. Schultz & Co., No. 9 Spruce Street, 1860).

Statement of the Revenue and Expense of the Main Line of the Public Works of Pennsylvania from 1830 to 1857, page 559.

Appendix D
2nd Pennsylvania Volunteer Infantry Unit, 1847 Company B Breakdown

(including 16 transfers)

Location	Number of Soldiers	Per-cent	Number Killed	Percent of Total Killed
Summit	46	52.8	14	58.3
Hollidaysburg	15	17.2	03	12.5
Pittsburgh	11	12.6	03	12.5
Blairsville	03	03.4	01	04.1
Newry	03	03.4	02	08.3
others	03	03.4	00	—
Armagh	02	02.2	01	04.1
Philadelphia	02	02.2	00	—
Johnstown	01	01.1	00	—
Unmarked	01	01.1	00	—
Total	87		24	27.5

—Percent killed 27.5% of total. Deaths by rank, 22 of 24 (or 91.6%) were privates; the two others were corporals. Number of wounded not counted.

Appendix E
Schedule No. 1
Western Division, Pennsylvania Rail Road
On and After August 31, 1851

EASTWARD		STATIONS	WESTWARD	
Passenger and Freight			Passenger and Freight	
Passenger Train No. 2			Passenger Train No.1	
P.M.	A.M.		A.M.	P.M.
6:15	10:15	CONEMAUGH	7:15	2:15
6:00	10:05	JOHNSTOWN	7:25	2:30
5:35	9:45	CONEMAUGH FURNACE	7:40	2:50
5:20	9:35	NINEVEH	7:50	3:03
4:55	9:15	NEW FLORENCE	8:10	3:30
4:30	9:00	LOCKPORT	8:30	3:50
P.M.	A.M.		A.M.	P.M.

H. H. HAUPT,
Gen'l Supt.

Source: *Triumph I, Altoona to Pitcairn 1846–1996* by Charles S. Roberts, assisted by Gary W. Schlerf (Baltimore: Barnard, Roberts and Co., Inc., 1997), p. 222.

Appendix F
Population of Cambria County, Pennsylvania, 1810–1900

Year	Population	Population Change
1810	2,117	—
1820	3,287	+55.26%
1830	7,076	+152.73%
1840	11,256	+59.08%
1850	17,773	+57.89%
1860	29,155	+64.04%
1870	36,569	+25.43%
1880	46,811	+28.01%
1890	66,375	+41.79%
1900	104,837	+57.94%

—Information, per U.S Census, 1810–1900

Appendix G
APRR Business Receipts

R. Humphreys 1839–50

Riffle & Humphreys Merchants 1846–51

Payroll Sheets APRR, 1844–57

Portage Rail Road October 1844

Wages Account To Sundries

Plane No 4

A. Westfall. Eng.	From June 1st to July 31st	61 ds @ $1.75 =	106.75
James Rhoads. Asst Eng	ditto	61 - @ 1.25 =	76.25
Thomas Carroll. Fireman	ditto	60¾ @ 1.12½	68.34
Philip McHenny. Helation	ditto	61 @ 1.00 =	61.00
E. Donaldson do	ditto	60¼ @ 1.00 =	60.25

Plane No 5

S. M. Brown Eng.	From June 1st to July 31st	61 ds @ $1.75 =	106.75
Daniel Walters Asst Eng	ditto	61 @ 1.25 =	76.25
Cornelius Dougherty Fireman	ditto	61 @ 1.12½	68.62½
Philip Campbell Helation	ditto	61 @ 1.00 =	61.00
Dominich Moon do	ditto	61 @ 1.00 =	61.00

Plane No 6

Philip Sanbolt Eng	From June 1st to July 31st	60 ds @ $1.75 =	105.00
Elisha Luckets Asst Eng	ditto	61 @ 1.25 =	76.25
Samuel P. Dushane Fireman	ditto	57 @ 1.12½	64.12½
David Powers Helation	ditto	61 @ 1.00 =	61.00
And. Purcell do	ditto	61 @ 1.00 =	61.00

Plane No 7

John McCaffry Eng.	From June 1st to July 31st	61 ds @ $1.75 =	106.75
John Humphrys Asst Eng	ditto	61 @ 1.25 =	76.25
Francis Wilhees Fireman	ditto	61 @ 1.12½	68.62½
Levi Basler Helation	ditto	61 @ 1.00 =	61.00
John Arged do	ditto	61 @ 1.00 =	61.00
William Humphrys d	ditto	61 @ 1.00 =	61.00

Plane No 8

Richard Thostler Eng.	From June 1st to July 31st	61 ds @ $1.75 =	106.75
Thos G. Dripps Asst Eng.	ditto	56¾ @ 1.25 =	70.93¾
Hugh O'Shely Fireman	ditto	61 @ 1.12½	68.62½
John McCurmich Helation	ditto	61 @ 1.00 =	61.00
John G. Lingelfalls do	ditto	61 @ 1.00 =	61.00

Plane No 10

Charles Cheney. Eng.	From Aug 1st to Sep 30th	61 ds @ $1.75 =	106.75
Thomas Flach. Asst Eng.	ditto	61 @ 1.25 =	76.25
Henry Caprolay. Fireman	ditto	61 @ 1.12½	68.62
Thomas Farroll. Helation	ditto	61 @ 1.00 =	61.00
James McFee do	ditto	61 @ 1.00 =	61.00 = 22

Original record courtesy of the Pennsylvania State Archives

ALLEGHENY PORTAGE RAILWAY, 1849.

Dr.

THE COMMONWEALTH OF PENNSYLVANIA,

To the following named persons for services at _Plane No. 6_

NAMES.	OCCUPATIONS.		NO. OF DAYS.	PRICE.	DOLLS.	CENTS.	Rec'd payment in full from Tho. J. Powrs, Sup. M.P.	Witness to signing by mark.
John McCloskey	Engineer	From the 1 day of Aug to the 31 day of Oct inclusive.	92	1.75	161	00	John McCloskey	
David Humphreys	off Engineer	From the 1 day of do to the 31 day of do inclusive.	92	1.25	115	00	Jacob Humphreys	
Thomas Humphreys	Fireman	From the 1 day of do to the 30 day of do inclusive.	91	1.10	102	37½	Thomas Humphreys	
George Marks	ditto	From the day of do to the day of do inclusive.	90	1.10	101	25	George Marks	
Hugh Jaylor	Watcher	From the day of do to the day of do inclusive.	92	1.00	92	00	Hugh Jaylor	
W. J. Haney	ditto	From the day of do to the day of do inclusive.	92	1.00	92	00	W J Haney	
John Rees		From the day of do to the day of do inclusive.	90	1.00	90	00	John Rees	
Michael McCorkle		From the day of .. to the .. day of do ..	92	1.00	92	00	Will McCorkle	
					835.62½			

Quant Sun COUNTY, SS:

Before me, a Justice of the Peace in and for said county, personally appeared the above named _John McCloskey_,

Foreman, who being lawfully qualified, saith that the above account is correct, and that neither of the above named persons were absent from the service of the Commonwealth during the time for which the above account is charged.

Sworn and subscribed, before me, _J. Humphreys_

this 5th day of _November_ 1849. } _John McCloskey_

I CERTIFY that I have examined the above Check Roll, and believe it to be correct.

Thos J Powrs
Supt. M. P.

Original record courtesy of the Pennsylvania State Archives

ALLEGHENY PORTAGE RAILWAY, 1850.

THE COMMONWEALTH OF PENNSYLVANIA,

To the following named persons for services at _Inclined Plane No 4._

Dr.

NAMES.	OCCUPATIONS.			NO. OF DAYS.	PRICE.	DOLLA.	CENTS.	Rec'd payment in full from W. S. Campbell, Sup. M. P.	Witness to signing by mark.
	Engineer	From the 1st day of _July_	to the 3rd day of _Aug_ inclusive.		1.75				Geo. C. Bell
	Conductor	From the ,, day of ,,	to the ,, day of ,, inclusive.		1.25				
	Fireman	From the ,, day of ,,	to the ,, day of ,, inclusive.		1.00				
	ditto	From the ,, day of ,,	to the ,, day of ,, inclusive.						
	fireman	From the ,, day of ,,	to the ,, day of ,, inclusive.						
	ditto	From the ,, day of ,,	to the ,, day of ,, inclusive.						
	ditto	From the ,, day of ,,	to the ,, day of ,, inclusive.		1.00				

_____ COUNTY, SS:

Before me, a Justice of the Peace in and for said county, personally appeared the above named
_____ Foreman, who being lawfully qualified, saith that the above account is correct, and that
neither of the above named persons were absent from the service of the Commonwealth during the time for which the
above account is charged.

Sworn and subscribed, before me,
this 14th day of _September_ 1850.

I CERTIFY that I have examined the above Check Roll, and believe it to be correct.

_____ Supt. M. P.

ALLEGHENY PORTAGE RAILWAY.

THE COMMONWEALTH OF PENNSYLVANIA

To *John Humphreys* DR.

1849		DOLLS.	CTS.
	For Services Rendered as State Agent from June 1st to August 31st 92 days at $1.50 per day	138	00

Cambria Cty Ss
Personally appeared before me a
Justice of the Peace in and for said County
John Humphreys who on his Oath says the
account as it stands stated is just and
true

Sworn & Subscribed
Novem 3d 1849

John Humphreys

RECEIVED, *November 3 rd* 1849, from THO. J. POWER, Superintendent of
Motive Power on the Allegheny Portage Railway, *One Hundred & Thirty eight*
dollars and ———— cents, the amount due on the above estimate.

$138.00   *John Humphreys*

I do certify that the above bill is correct, was had for, and applied to the use of the Commonwealth.

Tho. J. Power Supt. M. P.

Original record courtesy of the Pennsylvania State Archives

ALLEGHENY PORTAGE RAILROAD.

THE COMMONWEALTH OF PENNSYLVANIA,

To *John Humphreys* Dr.

		DOLLS.	CENTS.
For services rendered as *State Agent* from *Sep 1* to *November 30th* 184*9*, (both days inclusive) *91* days, at $ *1.50* per day.		*136*	*50*

Cambria COUNTY, SS:

PERSONALLY appeared before me, the subscriber, a Justice of the Peace in and for said county, —*John Humphreys* who being duly sworn according to law, saith the above account is correct,

SWORN and subscribed before me, this *28th* day of *December* 184*9*.

James McMichan

John Humphreys

RECEIVED, *December 28th* 184*9*, from THOS. J. POWER, Superintendent of Motive Power on the Allegheny Portage Railway, the sum set opposite my name in the above bill.

$ *136.57*

Cancel

Tho. J. Power

John Humphreys

Original record courtesy of the Pennsylvania State Archives

ALLEGHENY PORTAGE RAILROAD.

THE COMMONWEALTH OF PENNSYLVANIA,

To *Rolland Humphreys* DR.

1850.			DOLLS.	CENTS.
March	2	For 1 days hauling Materials with 3 horses 1 driver	2.	50
"	5th	For 1¾ days hauling Materials with 2 Horses		
		1 one driver @ $2.00	3.	50
			$6.00	

Cambria COUNTY, SS:

PERSONALLY appeared before me, the subscriber, a Justice of the Peace in and for said county,
Rolland Humphreys who being duly sworn according to law, saith the above account is correct.

Sworn and subscribed, before me, this

23ᵈ day of *May* 1850. } *R. Humphreys*

Ebensburg J.P.

RECEIVED, *May 23ᵈ* 1850, from W. S. CAMPBELL, Supervisor on the

Allegheny Portage Railway, *Six*

dollars and — cents, in full of the above bill. *R. Humphreys*

$ *6.00* *Correct*

Wm S Campbell Supr

Original record courtesy of the Pennsylvania State Archives

ALLEGHENY PORTAGE RAILWAY

THE COMMONWEALTH OF PENNSYLVANIA,

To *Riffel & Humphreys* Dr.

1850			DOLLS.	CTS.
June	1	For 250 Cords Wood delivered on Summit Level & Between plane No 4 & 5 @ $1.25 per Cord	250	00

RECEIVED, *June 12th* 1850, from W. S. Campbell, Superintendent of Motive Power on the Allegheny Portage Railway, *Two hundred & fifty*

dollars and ——————— cents, in full of the above bill.

•*250.00*

Riffel & Humphreys

I do certify that the above bill is correct, was had for, and applied to the use of the Commonwealth.

W. S. Campbell Supt

Original record courtesy of the Pennsylvania State Archives

CHECK ROLL.

Amount of labor of Horses and Drivers employed at hauling cars at the _Port of Plane No. 5_ of the Allegheny Portage Railroad, during

the month of _August_ 1850, at the rate of _Fifty_ cents per day per horse, and _Fifty_ cents per day per driver.

Rolland Humphrey CONTRACTOR.

	1	2	3	4	5	6	7	8	9	10	11	12	13	14	15	16	17	18	19	20	21	22	23	24	25	26	27	28	29	30	31	TOTAL.	CTS.	D'LS.	CTS.
HORSES.	4	4	4	.	.	4	4	4	4	4	.	4	4	4	4	4	4	.	4	4	4	4	4	4	4	4	4	4	4	4	4	108	50	54	00
DRIVERS.	1	1	1	.	1	1	1	1	1	1	.	1	1	1	1	1	1	.	.	1	1	1	1	1	1	1	1	1	1	1	1	27	50	13	50
																																		67	50

Cambria COUNTY, SS:

Before me, a Justice of the Peace for said county, came _Rolland Humphrey_

who being duly sworn, saith that the above account of time of horses and drivers employed in the

service of the Commonwealth, is correct.

SWORN and subscribed, before me, this _3rd_

day of _September_ 1850.

Lewis Hoggelow _A. Humphreys_

I CERTIFY that I have examined the above account, and believe the same to be correct.

Wm Campbell Supt

1850. _Sept 3rd_ Received of W. S. CAMPBELL, Superintendent of Transportation, _fifty seven_ dollars and _fifty_ cents, the above

amount, excepting the retained per centage; being

Paid, $ 67.50

Retained, $ —

$ 67.50

A. Humphreys

Original record courtesy of the Pennsylvania State Archives

CHECK ROLL.

Amount of labor of Horses and Drivers employed at hauling Cars at the _Foot of Plane No 3_ of the Allegheny Portage Railroad, during the month of _September_ 1850, at the rate of _Fifty_ cents per day per horse, and _Fifty_ cents per day per driver.

Welland Humphreys CONTRACTOR.

	1	2	3	4	5	6	7	8	9	10	11	12	13	14	15	16	17	18	19	20	21	22	23	24	25	26	27	28	29	30	31	TOTAL. CTS.	D'L'S. CTS.
HORSES.		4	4	4	4	4	4	4		4	4	4	4	4	4	4	4	4	4	4	4	4	4	4	4	4	4	4	4	4	4	100 50	$100.50
DRIVERS.		1	1	1	1	1	1	1		1	1	1	1	1	1	1	1	1	1	1	1	1	1	1	1	1	1	1	1	1	1	25 00	$25.00
																																	$125.50

Cambria COUNTY, SS: _Mr. Humphreys_

Before me, a Justice of the Peace for said county, came _Mr. Humphreys_ who being duly sworn, saith that the above account of time of horses and drivers employed in the service of the Commonwealth, is correct.

Sworn and subscribed, before me, this _day_ 1850. _Ro Humphreys_

day of _October first_ 1850.

Cambria J.P.

I CERTIFY that I have examined the above account, and believe the same to be correct.

Wm Campbell

1850. _October 1st_ Received of W. S. CAMPBELL, Superintendent of Transportation, _Sixty Two_ dollars and _75/100_ cents, the above amount, excepting the retained per centage ; being

Paid, $ _62.75_

Retained, $ _2.75_

     $ _2.75_

Ro Humphreys

CHECK ROLL.

Amount of labor of Horses and Drivers employed at hauling Cars at the Foot of Plane No. 1 of the Allegheny Portage Railroad, during the month of April 1850, at the rate of Fifty cents per day per horse, and Fifty cents per day per driver.

CONTRACTOR. *Willard Humphreys*

	1	2	3	4	5	6	7	8	9	10	11	12	13	14	15	16	17	18	19	20	21	22	23	24	25	26	27	28	29	30	31	TOTAL CTS.	D'LS CTS.
HORSES.																																100 50	50 00
DRIVERS.																																26 50	13 00
																																	$65 00

Cambria COUNTY, SS:

Before me, a Justice of the Peace for said county, came *Willard Humphreys* who being duly sworn, saith that the above account of time of horses and drivers employed in the service of the Commonwealth, is correct.

Sworn and subscribed, before me, this 23 day of May 1850. }

Willard Humphreys

Geo. Burgoon J.P.

I CERTIFY that I have examined the above account, and believe the same to be correct.

W. Campbell Supt

1850. March 23 Received of W. S. CAMPBELL, Superintendent of Transportation, Sixty five dollars and _____ cents, the above amount, excepting the retained per centage ; being

Paid, $ 85 00

Retained, $ ——

$ 65 00

Wm Humphreys

Original record courtesy of the Pennsylvania State Archives

CHECK ROLL.

Amount of labor of Horses and Drivers employed at hauling Cars at the _Foot of Plane_ ___ of the Allegheny Portage Railroad, during the month of _April_ 1850, at the rate of _fifty_ cents per day per horse, and _fifty_ cents per day per driver.

William Humphreys CONTRACTOR.

	1	2	3	4	5	6	7	8	9	10	11	12	13	14	15	16	17	18	19	20	21	22	23	24	25	26	27	28	29	30	31	TOTAL.	CTS.	D'LS.	CTS.
HORSES.	11	11	11	11	11	11	11	11	11	11	11	11	11	11	11		11	11	11	11		11	11	11	11	11	11	11	11	11		100	50	62	00
DRIVERS.	1	1	1	1	1	1	1		1	1	1	1	1	1	1		1	1	1	1	1	1	1	1	1	1	1	1	1	1		26	50	13	00
																																		$65 00	

Cambria COUNTY, SS:

Before me, a Justice of the Peace for said county, came _William Humphreys_ who being duly sworn, saith that the above account of time of horses and drivers employed in the service of the Commonwealth, is correct.

Sworn and subscribed, before me, this _23_ day of _May_ 1850. } _B. Humphreys_

Geo Burgoon, J.P.

I CERTIFY that I have examined the above account, and believe the same to be correct.

W. Campbell, Supt

Received of W. S. CAMPBELL, Superintendent of Transportation, _sixty five_ — dollars and — cents, the above amount, excepting the retained per centage ; being

Paid, $ _60.00_

Retained, $ ————

$ _65.00_

B. Humphreys

MERCHANTS WAY FREIGHT LINE,

(FORMERLY CALLED PICKWORTH & CO'S LINE,)

EXCLUSIVELY FOR THE TRANSPORTATION OF

 WAY FREIGHT

BETWEEN

PITTSBURGH, BLAIRSVILLE,

Johnstown, Hollidaysburg, Water Street,

And all intermediate places.

AGENTS,

C. A. M'ANULTY & Co. Canal Basin, Pittsburgh.

PICKWORTH & WOODS, Johnstown.   J. MILLER, Hollidaysburg.

Pittsburgh, *Nov 17* 184 *8*

Received of *Moore* the following packages, in apparent good order, marked as per margin, which we promise to transport by Canals and Rail Roads, and deliver in like order, (the dangers of the Rail Roads, and Canal navigation, Fire in Boats, Cars, and transhipping Depots, and incidental delays excepted, of which the certificate of a Superintendent, Collector or Lock-keeper, or the affidavit of a Boat Captain, or Car Master shall be evidence,) ...... on presentation of this receipt, and payment of freight, at ...... within ...... days, (Sundays excepted,) at the following rates per 100 lbs.

MARKS.	ARTICLES.	WEIGHT.
	+ C.P. *46* Flour	
	+ 1 bbl Sugar	263
	+ 1 box Starch	
	+ 4 kg Bar Lead Glass	160
	+ 3 Box Candles	165
	+ 4 " Soap	262
	+ 1 " Star Candles	32
	+ 1 " Cut Dry Sole	42
	+ 1/2 keg Toby	94
	+ 2 " W Lead	50
	+ 1 keg Gum	20
	+ 1 Ream Paper	15
	+ 2 Hay Forms	72
	+ 5 Smoothing Irons	27

Original record courtesy of the Pennsylvania State Archives

Messrs Riffle & Humphreys   *May 22d Holly Station 185_*

For Freight on   To **Pennsylvania Railroad Co.** Dr.

ARTICLES.	WEIGHT.	MARKS.	Dollars.	Cents.	FROM WHOM.
1 Keg M — 1 Box Candles					
1 Can " 2 " Soap					
1 Box Cheese	448	.55	2	47	
1 Box Dry Goods 1 Box Nuts					
½ Box Tobacco 1 Box Raisins					
2 Bundles Brooms	528	.70	3	70	
3 Reams Wrapping Paper	40	.45		18	
			6	35	

Rec Payment

Thomas Adcock

Original record courtesy of the Blair County Historical Society

ALLEGHENY PORTAGE RAIL ROAD.

The Commonwealth of Pennsylvania,

To *John Humphreys* Dr.

For services rendered as *Dispatcher Crifent* | DOLLARS. | CENTS.

from *July 1* to *July 31* 185 6,

(both days inclusive,) *31* days at $ *2.00* per day. $ *62.00*

Cambria COUNTY, *ss :*

Personally appeared before me, the subscriber, a Justice of the Peace in and for said county, *John Humphreys* who being duly sworn according to law, saith the above account is correct.

Sworn and subscribed before me this *4th*

day of *Septr* 185 *6* .

Wm Palmer J.P.

John Humphreys

RECEIVED *Sept 9* 185 *6* , from ~~John Ross,~~ *Wm Calahan* Superintendent of Motive Power on the Allegheny Portage Railway, *sixty Two* dollars

and ———— cents, the amount of the above bill in full.

John Humphreys

I certify the above bill to be correct.

Wm S Calahan

Superintendent Motive Power.

Original record courtesy of the Pennsylvania State Archives

Notes

Chapter One
The Cambrians
1. Fourth U.S. Census, Cambria County, Pa., 1820.
2. *Ebensburg Sky*, July 4, 1833, p. 3.

Chapter Two
The Allegheny Portage Railroad
1. Taylor, *The Transportation Revolution 1815–1860*, p. 43.
2. Colemann, *The Disruption of Pennsylvania Democracy, 1848–1860*, pp. 13–14.
3. Ibid.
4. Wilson, *The Evolution, Decadence and Abandonment of the Allegheny Portage Railroad*, pp. 289–305.
5. Charles Treziyulney—third Commissioner, Board of Canal Commissioners, Report to Governor of Pennsylvania, February 21, 1825.
6. Wilson, *The Evolution, Decadence and Abandonment of the Allegheny Portage Railroad*, pp. 289–305.
7. Burgess and Kennedy, *The Centennial History of the Pennsylvania Railroad Company*, 1949, p. 10.
8. Sylvester Welch's Report on the Allegheny Portage Railroad, 1833.
9. Engineer Moncure Robinson report, November 21, 1829.
10. Wilson, *The Evolution, Decadence and Abandonment of the Allegheny Portage Railroad*, pp. 289–305.
11. Jacobs, *The Juniata Canal and Old Portage RR*, p. 10.
12. Skew Arch Marker along Old Route 22, near Plane No. 6, Blair County, erected in 1928, south side of monument.
13. Sylvester Welch's Report on the Allegheny Portage Railroad, 1833.
14. Blair County Historical Society, Portage RR Files.
15. Sylvester Welch's Report on the Allegheny Portage Railroad, 1833.

Chapter Three
The Operation of the Portage
1. *Reminiscences of the First Railroad over the Allegheny Mountain*, Read before the Historical Society of Pennsylvania April 8, 1878, by Solomon Roberts.
2. Story, *History of Cambria County, Pa.*, 1907, p. 365.
3. Baumgardner and Hoenstine, *The Allegheny Old Portage Railroad 1834–1854*, p. 62.
4. Jacobs, *The Juniata Canal and Old Portage Railroad*, p. 16.
5. Pennsylvania State Archives, Board of Canal Commissioners Files, Allegheny Portage RR Day Book, 1839–1841. Work based on normal work day (between Incline Planes Nos. 7 and 8), August 1839. Average 174.85 Cars per day (Mon. to Sat.), but only average of 17.5 Cars on Sundays (between Incline Planes Nos. 7 and 8), during August 1839.

6. Wilson, *The Evolution, Decadence and Abandonment of the Allegheny Portage Railroad*, pp. 289–305.

7. *Reminiscences of the First Railroad over the Allegheny Mountain*, Read before the Historical Society of Pennsylvania April 8, 1878, by Solomon Roberts.

8. *History of the Pennsylvania Railroad Co.*, 1898, p. 123.

9. *The Canal and Portage Register*, July 27, 1836.

10. Wilson, *The Evolution, Decadence and Abandonment of the Allegheny Portage Railroad*, pp. 298–305.

11. "Canal Circular," by Thomas L. Wilson, Sec., Board of Canal Commissioners, dated February 7, 1842.

12. In 1849, one of the biggest years on the Portage, they represented only 4.3% of all tonnage traffic.

13. Wilson, *The Evolution, Decadence and Abandonment of the Allegheny Portage Railroad*, pp. 298–305.

14. Not necessarily true. Records from 1839 and 1851 indicate that the Board of Canal Commissioners authorized such night hauls to speed up work.

15. Story, *History of Cambria County, Pa.*, 1907, pp. 354–55.

16. Charles Dickens, *American Notes*, 1842, pp. 178–79.

17. Burgess and Kennedy, *Centennial History of the Pennsylvania Railroad Company, 1846–1946*, p. 92.

18. *The Canal and Portage Register*, December 7, 1836, p. 2.

19. Story, *History of Cambria County, Pa.*, 1907, p. 365.

Chapter Four
Contacts and Contracts

1. Henry V. Poor, American Railroad Journal Report, 1860, p. 559.

2. Pennsylvania State Archives, Board of Canal Commissioners Files, Allegheny Portage Day Book, 1839–1841, and Blair County Hist. Society, Portage RR Records,.

3. Pennsylvania State Archives, Board of Canal Commissioners Files, Allegheny Portage Day Book, 1839–1841, and Blair County Hist. Society.

4. Based upon 6¼ cents per car in 1839.

5. Cambria County Register of Deeds, Deed Vol. 9, pp. 763–65.

6. Burgess and Kennedy, *Centennial History of the Pennsylvania Railroad Company, 1846–1946*, p. 92.

7. Taylor, *The Transportation Revolution 1815–1860*, p. 162.

8. Pennsylvania State Archives, Board of Canal Commissioners Files, Payroll Sheets.

Chapter Five
Wheels of Peace — Wheels of War

1. John White Geary was assistant superintendent and engineer of the APRR in 1846. After forming an infantry unit and becoming its captain in late 1846, he was elected to lieutenant colonel, and later colonel of the 2nd Pa. Vol. Inf. in the Mexican War, Colonel Geary served under Gen. Winfield Scott until 1848. Geary was later governor of Kansas in the 1850s, and Pennsylvania in the late 1860s.

2. Story, *History of Cambria County, Pa.*, 1907, p. 7.

3. American Highlanders Letter, Blair County Historical Society, Portage RR Records.

4. *Johnstown Transcript*, May 14, 1849, p. 3.

5. *Mountain-Sentinel*, May 26, 1849, p. 3, col. 3.

6. *Mountain-Sentinel*, July 12, 1849, p. 3, col. 2.

7. *Mountain-Sentinel*, July 19, 1849.

8. *Mountain-Sentinel*, August 2, 1849, p. 3, col. 1.

Chapter Six
Riffle & Humphreys Merchants

1. Pennsylvania State Archives, Board of Canal Commissioners Files, GS-17.

2. Freight Receipt to "Riffle & Humphreys Merchants," dated November 17, 1848.

3. Pennsylvania State Archives, Board of Canal Commissioners Files, GS-17.

4. "Villa Nova College" Letter, Blair County Historical Society, Portage RR Files.

5. "Noon" Letter, Blair County Historical Society, Portage RR Files.

6. Jacobs, *The Juniata Canal and Old Portage Railroad*, p. 15.

7. Seventh U.S. Census, Cambria County, Pa., 1850.

8. Deed: Cambria County Deed Book, Deed Vol. 9, pp. 423–24.

9. Pennsylvania State Archives, Board of Canal Commissioners Files, GS-17.

10. Pennsylvania State Archives, Board of Canal Commissioners, GS-17.

11. *Mountain-Sentinel*, May 6, 1852, p. 4, col. 4.

12. Pennsylvania State Archives, Board of Canal Commissioners, GS-17.

Chapter Seven
The Summit Mansion Hotel

1. "Lemon House and Coal Mine," p. 13; Also, Sesquicentennial of Cambria County, Thomas J. Chapman, The Valley of the Conemaugh (Altoona, 1865), p. 86; and the *Ebensburg Sky*, December 4, 1833, p. 2.

2. From *Altoona Mirror*, newspaper article, March 15, 1980.

3. Blair County Historical Society, Summit Mansion House Register Book/Ledger Book.

4. Deed: Cambria County Recorders Office, Deed Vol. 14, pp. 737–39.

5. Seventh U.S. Census, Cambria Co., Pa., 1850.

6. *Mountain-Sentinel*, January 23, 1851, p. 3, col. 5.

7. *Mountain-Sentinel*, June 17, 1852, p. 2, col. 1.

8. Blair County Historical Society, Summit Mansion House files, and "The Allegheny Old Portage Railroad 1834–1854," pp. 22–35.

9. *The World Book* (1928 Edition), Vol. 6, p. 3449.

10. Story, *History of Cambria County, Pa.*, 1907, p. 356.

11. Deed: Cambria County Recorders Office, Deed Vol. 14, pp. 737–39.

Chapter Eight
Accidents and Snake Heads

1. Composite of several newspapers from 1833 to 1857, including: *The Canal and Portage Register, Hollidaysburg Register, & Huntingdon County Inquirer, Mountain-Sentinel*.

2. *Mountain-Sentinel*, 1850 and 1851 editions.

3. *Hollidaysburg Register, & Inquirer*, September 2, 1846, p. 3, col. 2.

4. Composite of 1850 newspaper articles including: 17. *Hollidaysburg Register & Blair County Inquirer*, April 24, 1850, p. 3, col. 2; *Hollidaysburg Register, & Inquirer*, April 24, 1850, p. 3, col. 2; *Hollidaysburg Register, & Inquirer*, May 1, 1850, p. 3, col. 2; *Hollidaysburg Register, & Inquirer*, July 24, 1850, p. 3, col. 3, and Note to Wm S. Campbell, Supt. Motive Power Division of the APRR 1850, Blair County Hist. Society, Baker Mansion Portage RR Papers, and *Mountain-Sentinel*, September 26, 1850.

5. *Hollidaysburg Register, & Inquirer*, October 6, 1841, p. 3, col. 1.

6. *Hollidaysburg Register, & Inquirer*, Sept. 1, 1847, p. 3, col. 3.

7. *Mountain-Sentinel*, Thursday, September 26, 1850.

8. *Hollidaysburg Register, & Inquirer*, July 24, 1850, p. 3, col. 3,.

9. *Hollidaysburg Register, & Inquirer*, May 12, 1852, p. 3, col. 2.

10. *Hollidaysburg Register, & Huntingdon County Inquirer*, November 2, 1836, p. 3, col. 2.

11. *Mountain-Sentinel*, July 12, 1849, p. 3, col. 2.

12. Jacobs, *The Juniata Canal and Old Portage Railroad*, p. 11.

13. Blair Co. Hist. Society, Summit Mansion Hotel Register, June 28, 1852,.

Chapter Nine
The Pennsylvania Railroad Company

1. Henry Poor, American Railroad Journal Report, 1860.

2. "Chesapeake and Ohio Canal Handbook," p. 15.

3. Hollis and Roberts, *East End, B&O's "Neck of the Bottle,"* p. 15.

4. Ibid.

5. Jacobs, *The Juniata Canal and Old Portage Railroad*, p. 15.

6. Pennsylvania State Archives, Board of Canal Commissioners Files; Payroll sheets.

7. Cambria County, Pa., Tax Rolls, 1833–1860.

8. Word, *J. Edgar Thomson, Master of the Pennsylvania*, pp. 81–82.

9. Story, *History of Cambria County, Pa.*, 1907, p. 364.

10. *Mountain-Sentinel*, December 18, 1851, p. 2, col. 1.

11. McCullough, *The Johnstown Flood*, pp. 45–47.

12. Word, *J. Edgar Thomson, Master of the Pennsylvania*, pp. 81–82.

13. *Mountain-Sentinel*, December 18, 1851, p. 2, col. 1.

14. Wilson, *The Evolution, Decadence and Abandonment of the Allegheny Portage Railroad*, pp. 289–305.

Chapter Ten
Death in the Staple Bend Tunnel

1. Blair Co. Hist. Society, September 9, 1851, Summit Mansion Hotel Registration Book.

2. Blair County Historical Society, Portage RR Records.

3. *Mountain-Sentinel*, June 17, 1852, p. 2, col. 1.

4. Blair Co. Hist. Society, Summit Mansion Hotel Registration Book, June 12, 1852.

5. Blair Co. Hist. Society, Summit Mansion Hotel Registration Book, June 28, 1852,.

6. *Mountain-Sentinel*, July 8, 1852,.

7. Lloyds Cemetery headstone, "Humphreys Rowland – born in Wales – died 1852 – Killed at the Allegheny Portage R. Road Tunnel."

8. Cambria County Orphans Court, filed and probated in 1853.

Chapter Eleven
The "New" Portage Railroad

1. *The Transportation Revolution*, p. 162.

2. Henry Poor, *American Railroad Journal Report*, 1860, p. 559.

3. Ibid.

4. *Mountain-Sentinel*, Thursday, May 5, 1853, p. 2, col. 1.

5. Wilson, *The Evolution, Decadence and Abandonment of the Allegheny Portage Railroad*, pp. 289–305.

6. Roberts, *Triumph I, Altoona to Pitcairn, 1846–1996*, p. 279.

7. Burgess and Kennedy, *Centennial History of the Penn RR Co.*, p. 81.

8. "Map of the Pennsylvania Rail Road, from Harrisburg to Pittsburgh, and of the Columbia & Lancaster & Harrisburg R.R.s from Philadelphia to Harrisburg. H. Haupt, Chf. Eng., J. P. & Lesley, Jr. Topographers, J. G. Shoemaker, engr., Philadelphia, Pa., 1855."

9. Story, *History of Cambria County, Pa.*, 1907, pp. 359–60.

10. Ibid.

11. Henry Poor, American Railroad Journal Report, 1860.

12. Alexander, *The Pennsylvania Railroad, A Pictorial History*, p. 169.

13. Contracts: Pennsylvania State Archives, Board of Canal Commissioners Files.

14. Ibid.

15. A Citizen of Adams County, Sale of the Main Line, Letter No. IX.

Chapter Twelve
The End of the Line!

1. Pennsylvania State Archives, Board of Canal Commissioners, Correspondence 1857.

2. Burgess and Kennedy, *Centennial History of the Penn RR Co. 1846–1946*, p. 711.

3. Ibid.

4. Henry V. Poor, ARJ Report, 1860, pp. 558–59.

Epilogue

1. *Cambria Freeman*, July 27, 1872, p. 3, col. 2.

2. John W. Humphreys article, *Greensburg Newspaper*, Derry Social News, 1920s.

3. Anderson, *Robert E. Peary and the Fight for the North Pole*, pp. 11–23.

Bibliography

Books

Alexander, Edwin P. *The Pennsylvania Railroad, A Pictorial History*. New York: W. W. Norton and Co., Inc., 1947, pp. 168–69.

Anderson, Madelyn Klein. *Robert E. Peary and the Fight for the North Pole*. New York: Justin Books Ltd., 1992, pp. 11–23.

Baumgardner, Mahlon J. and Floyd G. Hoenstine. *The Allegheny Old Portage Railroad 1834–1854*, Building, Operation and Travel between Hollidaysburg and Johnstown Pennsylvania. Ebensburg, Pa., pp. 9–35, Copyright 1952, reprinted 1985.

Burgess, George H. and Miles C. Kennedy. *Centennial History of the Pennsylvania Railroad Company, 1846–1946*, of Coverdale & Colpitts, The Pennsylvania Railroad Company, Philadelphia, Pa., 1949.

Colemann, John F. "The Disruption of Pennsylvania Democracy, 1848–1860," pp. 13–14, Pennsylvania Historical and Museum Commission, Harrisburg, Pa., 1975.

Dickens, Charles. *American Notes*, chapter 10. Some Further Account of the Canal Boat, Its Domestic Economy, and Its Passengers. Journey to Pittsburg Across the Allegheny Mountains. Pittsburg, 1842, pp. 178 and 179.

Grant, Ulysses S. *The Personal Memoirs of U.S. Grant*, published by C. L. Webster, New York, originally printed 1885 and 1886, reprinted by Penguin Books 1999, Chapter 2.

Hollis, Jeffrey R., and Charles S. Roberts. *East End, B&O's "Neck of the Bottle" Harpers Ferry to Cumberland 1842–1992*. Baltimore, Md.: Barnard, Roberts and Co., Inc., 1992, p. 15.

Jacobs, Harry A., *The Juniata Canal and Old Portage Railroad*, Past President, The Blair County Historical Society, Hollidaysburg, Pa., originally September 20, 1941, reprinted 1969.

Levy, Benjamin. *Lemon House and Coal Mine*. National Park Service, U. S. Dept. of Interior, January 31, 1968, p. 13.

McCullough, David. *The Johnstown Flood*. New York: Simon & Schuster, Inc., 1968; reprinted 1987, p. 47.

Poor, Henry V., Esq., Editor of the *American Railroad Journal. History of the Railroads and Canals of the United States of America, Exhibiting Their Progress, Cost, Revenues, Expenditures & Present Condition*. 3 vols. — vol. 1., New York: John H. Schultz & Co., No. 9 Spruce Street, 1860; Reprinted 1970. Statement of the Revenue and Expense of the Main Line of the Public Works of Pennsylvania from 1830 to 1857, p. 559.

Roberts, Charles S., assisted by Gary W. Schlerf. *Triumph I, Altoona to Pitcairn, 1846–1996*. Baltimore, Md.: Barnard, Roberts and Co., Inc., June 1997, p. 279.

Roberts, Solomon W. *Reminiscences of the First Railroad over the Allegheny Mountain*, read before the Historical Society of Pennsylvania April 8, 1878. Reprinted from *The Pennsylvania Magazine of History and Biography*, vol. 11, no. 4, 1878.

Story, Henry Wilson. *History of Cambria County Pennsylvania*, with Genealogical Memoirs, illustrated vol. 2 (3 vols.), New York and Chicago: The Lewis Publishing Company, 1907, p. 651.

Tanner, Henry S. *A Description of the Canals and Railroads of the United States Comprehending Notices of all the works of internal Improvements through the Several States* [1840]. New York: Tanner & J. Disturnell, 1840, p. 129, reprinted 1970.

Taylor, George Rogers. *The Transportation Revolution 1815–1860*, vol. 4, The Economic History of the United States. New York: Holt, Rinehart and Winston, c. 1951, chaps. 1–4.

Ward, James A. *J. Edgar Thomson, Master of the Pennsylvania*. Westport, Conn.: Greenwood Press, 1980, pp. 81–82.

Welch, Sylvester. *Allegheny Portage Railroad*, 1833 Report. Gettysburg, Pa.: Thomas Publications, June 1988.

Wilson, William Bender. *The Evolution, Decadence and Abandonment of the Allegheny Portage Railroad*. The Pennsylvania Railroad

Men's News (Philadelphia, Pa.), Sept. 1897, vol. 9: pp. 289–305; Oct. 1897, vol. 9: pp. 317–23.

——. *History of the Pennsylvania Railroad Co.* Philadelphia, Pa.: H. T. Cortes & Co., 1899, p. 123.

The World Book. Chicago: W. F. Quarrie & Co., 1928, vol. 6, p. 3449.

Articles
Memoirs, Diaries, Journals

A Citizen of Adams County. *Sale of the Main Line, Letters on the Subject of the Sale of the Main Line of the Public Improvements owned by the Commonwealth of Pennsylvania.* Originally Published in the Philadelphia *Evening Bulletin.* Philadelphia: McLaughlin Brothers' Book and Job Printing Office, Bulletin Building, 1857.

"Humphreys & Riffle Merchants," business papers, Blair County Historical Society, Baker Mansion, Altoona, Pa.

Private Blair, Mexican War Diary 1846–48, Cambria County Historical Society, Ebensburg, Pa.

"Souvenir of Loretto Centenary: 1799–1899," by Swope Bros., Printers, Cresson, Pa., October 10, 1899, p. 180.

Summit Mansion Hotel Ledgers, Blair County Historical Society, Baker Mansion, Altoona, Pa.

Newspapers and Magazines

Cambria Freeman, Ebensburg, Pa.

The Canal and Portage Register, Hollidaysburg, Pa.

Democrat and Sentinel, Ebensburg, Pa.

Ebensburg Mountain Sentinel, Ebensburg, Pa.

The Ebensburg Sky, Ebensburg, Pa.

Historic Society of Pennsylvania Magazine, Harrisburg, Pa.

The Hollidaysburg Register, & Huntingdon County Inquirer, Hollidaysburg, Pa.

Mountain-Sentinel, Ebensburg, Pa.

The Weekly Tribune-Johnstown, Johnstown, Pa.

Booklets

"Chesapeake and Ohio Canal," Official National Park Handbook #142, U.S Department of the Interior, National Park Service, Washington, D. C., 1991.

Smith, Larry D. with individual contributions authored by others, *150th Anniversary History of Blair County, Pennsylvania*, by Larry D. Smith with individual contributions authored by others. Apollo, Pa.: Closson Press, 1997.

Index

— The Author —

CHRISTOPHER J. LEWIE is an award-winning city planner from Columbus, Ohio. His book *Two Generations on the Allegheny Portage Railroad* is the true story of the first railroad to cross the Allegheny Mountains in western Pennsylvania in 1834 and two generations of men (the Humphreys) who worked on it for 25 years until 1857. The Humphreys were also his direct ancestors from Wales. Mr. Lewie also worked as a researcher and on-screen personality for the documentary film "Lost Legend: The Chic Harley Story."

— COVER ILLUSTRATION —

CROSSING OF THE ALLEGHANY, PENNSYLVANIA RAILROAD

Railroad Museum of Pennyslvania

Pennsylvania Historical and Museum Commission

WHITE MANE PUBLISHING CO., INC.

To Request a Catalog Please Write to:

WHITE MANE PUBLISHING COMPANY, INC.

P.O. Box 708 • Shippensburg, PA 17257

e-mail: marketing@whitemane.com

Breinigsville, PA USA
20 March 2011
258013BV00006B/1/P